This is
FAST CRUISING

This is
FAST CRUISING

Peter Johnson

NAUTICAL

also by Peter Johnson
Passage Racing
Ocean Racing and Offshore Yachts
Yachtsman's Guide to the Rating Rule
Yachting World Handbook
Boating Britain
Guinness Book of Yachting Facts and Feats
Offshore Manual International
Guinness Guide to Sailing

First published in Great Britain 1985 by
NAUTICAL BOOKS
an imprint of Conway Maritime Press Ltd
24 Bride Lane, Fleet Street
London EC4Y 8DR

ISBN 0 85177 347 8

Filmset in The Netherlands
Printed in Italy

Acknowledgements

Line drawings by Ray Harvey MRINA BSc CEng

My thanks are due to all those with whom I have sailed over the years, either on my own boats or on others who have contributed ideas found in these pages. Material on storm techniques and experiments has additionally been obtained from Jim Robson-Scott (Australia) and D.J. Jordan (USA), whose articles appeared in *Sail*. On short-handed sailing, contributions have been made by Dick Everitt and Geoff Hales (UK). Electronic position finding and especially future developments have had input from Basil d'Oliveira (UK). Dick Koopmans (Holland) made suggestions and points in a number of chapters.

Wim de Bruijn (Holland) the editor, and other colleagues in United Nautical Publishers (in Italy and Germany) have assisted at every stage.

The majority of the photographs are the work of Patrick Roach (UK) who has spent much time checking his files and taking special shots for the book.

Photographic credits
Patrick Roach
1.1, 1.2, 1.6, 1.7, 1.9, 1.10, 1.14, 1.15, 1.16, 2.1, 2.2, 2.3, 2.4, 3.7, 3.9, 4.1, 4.2, 4.3, 4.4, 4.5, 4.6, 4.7, 5.2, 5.3, 5.4, 5.7, 5.8, 5.9, 6.2, 7.2, 7.7, 8.9, 10.1, 10.2, 10.4. Heading shots chapters 1,2,5 & 10. Alastair Black 1.3, 1.4 and heading shot chapter 9. John Ridgway 1.5, Theo Kampa 2.5, Alan Watts 6.3, Colin Jarman 9.2 and heading shot chapter 7, Geoff Hales 9.1, Koren Evans 9.3, *Yachting World* 7.6.

All other photographs are by the author.

NOTE. A mile when mentioned is always the *nautical mile.* 1 international nautical mile = 1852 metres = 6067 feet.

Contents

Introduction: why fast cruising?

Once it was easy to cruise swiftly. You bought a not-too-old racing yacht and away you went, making rings round the traditional cruiser.

Now that is no longer practical, for in the 80s, we are in one of these periods where the cruising and racing species of sailing yacht have diverged. In the early part of this century large cruising yachts could cross the oceans (like commercial or naval sailing vessels); and small cruisers resembled fishing boats, for instance with deep concave sheer (to haul nets). Racing boats were for inshore use only, skimming dishes and local one-designs: even large yachts raced on closed courses in protected waters.

When between the wars ocean racing made its appearence, the competitors were at first heavy traditional boats such as American schooners, or European pilot cutters. By the early thirties special designs for ocean racing appeared. They had the habitability of cruising yachts, yet aimed for the speed of the racer; though their performance was markedly inferior to the inshore racer, such as the metre boat or one-design.

These ocean racers made good fast cruisers. Indeed a number still sail today. A major definitive series of books on sport had one volume called 'Cruising and Ocean Racing' because the techniques were so similar.

In the 50s and 60s came light displacement and boats specially built to rating rules, yet these were the times when 'today's racer is tomorrow's cruiser'. Cruising men accepted the lighter faster boats; again many of the offshore racers of this period are still in use as cruisers.

In 1970 came a world rule and also by this time the old One Ton Cup, previously used for inshore 6-metre boats was put to use for ocean racers sailing Olympic as well as offshore courses. The flat-out offshore racer was on its way! For a while some of the racers still made practical cruisers, but the polarization of racing classes at 'Ton Cup' and other big series (Sardinia, Admiral's Cup,

SORC) and the arrival of 'hi-tech' materials meant the winning racer became unconvertable for cruising. The scene below decks (more like the inside of an aircraft wing than a cabin), the slim rigs, the big sail areas, the flush deck layout and lack of cockpit except for the helmsman: such features are not for cruising.

On the other side of the coin, cruisers are being developed with rig systems that are not allowed when racing and accommodation and hull shape uncompetitive with the extreme needs of modern racing. Thus sailing cruisers and offshore racers after a marriage between about 1935 and 1975 are again far apart in type and purpose.

There are boats which are exceptions and some of these have stemmed from the single and two handed international races. At first these racers were intended to allow 'ordinary yachts' to race without big crews and expensive gear. But they have over the years bred their own version of hi-tech, sometimes giant specialist and sponsored craft. Among the fleets there are also more moderate and easily handled vessels, which *are* suitable for cruising and these can be searched for lessons for the fast cruiser.

When I sail I like to do so fast and efficiently. Once it was possible to test ones ability on the race course between cruises: now for reasons carefully explained above, that is no longer a proposition. Here then is the philosophy of fast cruising. In a way we have to compete against ourselves – cruising which is smart, satisfying. It is also sailing-ish, that means not switching on the motor for every head wind or light air!

If you like to have everything exactly right on board so that reefing and docking, or cooking and sleeping at sea, happen smoothly and enjoyably, then it is all part of what I choose to call fast cruising. The main features of fast cruising for one person will be different to those of another, but in this book are ideas and reminders for those who already actively sail and cruise. Perhaps fast cruising is a combination of a number of ways of getting it just right in one's own sailing. Anyway this is fast cruising.

1. What makes for fast cruising

When a maxi ocean racer some 80 ft (24.3 m) sweeps past you at sea it is an impressive sight. Size, power, speed made our efforts in a 35 ft fast cruiser (10.7 m), which until then we thought were noteworthy, look puny. One of my crew, who had waved to the people on the maxi without response, decided they had got it wrong. 'What is the point', he said, 'of building a huge boat with the object of going so fast, that she spends less and less time at sea?'. I decided to defend the magnificent sailing vessel, pointing out that the other side of this coin was that those who sail her could cover much more distance in an equivalent time. After all, though our time is limited, we can sail any distance on the seas of this world.

Sailing yachts are basically a slow method of transport. So of course are all waterborne vessels, but under sail there are the additional no-go factors of calm and head winds. Thus for weekend and holiday cruising, the cruising range is limited and by definition monotonous. From your home port, you can only sail so far; and again your sailing is relatively limited at the weekend or the next holiday. Depending on your home waters or what lies just beyond them, what is the fun of this after a few years? There are ways of outflanking this natural restriction, which include the following. (1) *Chartering,* fly to somewhere a thousand miles away or more and enjoy a new cruising ground; (2) Owning a *large yacht with permanent crew* that can take her to chosen waters for the owner and his friends to join; it is for those who can afford it and the 'maxi' comes into this category; (3) at the other end of the scale, a small *trailer-sailer* can be towed behind a car to a new piece of coastline (P 1.1) (4) *race* the boat offshore, or inshore so that the cruising ground and an-chorages become of secondary importance; (5) retire or take enough time off to make an *extended voyage,* which may be along coast or across oceans; (6) sail a *multihull* of a type with such high average speed that cruising range is extended. (P 1.2)

Many cruising people may not wish to partake in any of these 'solutions', or may be unable to do so; thus it remains logical to improve the speed of their own cruising in an existing boat or by having a more suitable boat. It is worth recalling the distances in nautical miles that can be achieved at certain speeds. (Fig 1.1). These distances are further reduced, though pleasantly enough, by putting into harbour every 150 miles. A stay in harbour of 18 hours is equivalent to a passage of 90 miles at 5 knots, though in practice much time is lost in diverting to make port (see below). So we see that a 48 hour weekend with one port of call gives a

11

NAUTICAL MILES	DIRECT PASSAGE			PORT EVERY 150 MILES		
	4 knots	5½ knots	7 knots	4 knots	5½ knots	7 knots
60	15 h	11h	8½h	15 h	11h	8½h
150	37½h	27h	21 h	37½h	27h	21 h
300	75 h	54h	42 h	93 h	72h	60 h
750	7d 19 h	5d 16h	4d 11 h	10d 19 h	8d 16h	7d 19 h
1000	10d 9 h	7d 14h	5d 22 h	14d 21 h	12d 2h	10d 10 h

Fig. 1.1 Distances that can be achieved at yacht speeds over cruising times available. Distances are shown both direct and if putting into port for 18 hours every 150 miles.

range of 75 miles at 5 knots average. A two week holiday using the same criteria for calling at ports gives a *range* of 550 miles at the same average and assuming the yacht has to return to her home port. (Range is half the distance actually sailed: it is 'there and back'.)

Actual yacht speeds

Records exist for passages by racing boats or boats specially set up to break speed records. The fastest sailing boat in the world is *Crossbow II* at 36.0 knots, achieved over a measured distance of 500 m (1640 ft) in 1980: at the time of writing (1985) this has not been bettered. Also in the high speed category are sail boards and in 1983, over the same measured distance one of these got to 30.82 knots. (Fred Haywood). Both these craft hardly relate to cruising yachts; in fact the only things they have in common is that they sit on the water (just) and are propelled by wind. *Crossbow II* is an

1.1 Extend the range by trailer-sailing.

asymmetrical catamaran, that sails fast with the wind abeam on the starboard side only and the sail board was short, ultra-light and had a carbon-fibre wing mast. These boats only have to keep up such average speeds for less than a minute. (P 1.3)

The fastest recorded passage unsurprisingly was by a very specialist vessel, but she did have to carry crew, stores and at least minimal equipment. The speed was 12.94 knots and the boat was the foiled trimaran *Jet Services* sailed by Patrick Morvan (France) from Sandy Hook off New York harbour to the Lizard Point in south west England (2925 miles in 8 days 16 hours 33 minutes 17 seconds). (P

1.2 Highest speeds at sea, but hardly cruising.

1.4). Below this there are a whole host of records and some of these are useful markers when considering fast cruising speeds. An example of a conventional but very large racing yacht (79 ft, 24 m) with a large crew is John Kilroy's (USA) *Kialoa* in the 630 mile Sydney to Hobart race in 1975 recording 10.1 knots. An older boat on a shorter course was *Stella Polare*, (61 ft, 18.6 m) sailed by Giancarlo Basile (Italy) in the Giraglia race in the Mediterranean at 8.38 knots in 1975. The 41.1 ft (12.5 m) *Ocean Bound* was sailed single handed round the world with several

1.3 Built to sail at speed for just 500 metres, Mayfly at 23 knots.

1.5 English Rose VI *sailed round the world non-stop at an average of 6.48 knots.*

stops in 1979-1980 by David Scott-Cowper (Britain) at an average of 5.45 knots. The fastest non-stop sail around the world (Scotland and back via all southern capes) was by John Ridgway and Andy Briggs

English Rose VI (56.1 ft, 17.1 m) in 1983-84 in 193 days averaging 6.48 knots (P 1.5). Both these last mentioned boats were conventional fast cruisers; they were not flat out racers, nor did they have large crews (they were crewed by one and two men only respectively). Both were trying to get a move on within the limitations of the conditions; neither could run the engine for any length of time (if at all). The figures give us a clue to average speeds over a period. Using the same figures and assuming the ends of the boats are of a proportion (because length overall, LOA, has been quoted) it gives average speeds as follows

40 ft	12.2 m	5.4 knots
35 ft	10.7 m	5.3 knots
30 ft	9.1 m	4.9 knots
25 ft	7.6 m	4.5 knots

These are approximate average speeds based on these long voyages of short handed persons. Maximum speeds are another matter altogether and for a modern fast cruiser these might be in the region of the square root of the length of the waterline in feet times a constant of between 1.5 and 1.7. Taking a 40 ft (12.2 m) boat as above, this gives at 1.6 ratio a maximum speed of 9 knots (waterline assumed at 32 ft (9.8 m)), but we know that our speedometers have clocked higher than this running before a strong wind down big waves, but such surges last only for short bursts. The average speed of a fast cruiser in knots equals the square root of the waterline in feet (e.g. 32 ft yacht with 25 ft waterline will average 5 knots). In metric 1.8 times square root of waterline in metres equals average speed in

1.4 Jet Services: *fastest across the Atlantic.*

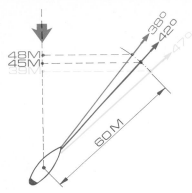

Fig 1.2 How sailing close to the wind improves actual distance made to windward.

knots. These figures which are only guides, do not apply to exotic craft such as multihulls or ultra-light displacement boats, known as ULDBs.

What uses up time
The nature of an average is that some of the time passages will be at a higher speed and at other times lower. In passage making a number of incidents conspire to slow things down. For any given boat, these are as follows. (1) *Head winds.* Once the yacht can no longer lay the course, she is sailing extra distance and possibly slower through the water. Windward ability is more important to cruising yachts than racing yachts, for downwind courses present no basic problems and the extra half a knot when off the wind is of little interest to the cruiser. Racers may wish to sacrifice windward performance very slightly in order to be more effective with fancy down-wind sails. The answer to head winds is to sail really close and fast to windward. Modern yachts over 30 ft (9.1 m) (small boats are inherently less weatherly especially in a seaway), should be expected to sail at 28 degrees to the apparent wind in a slight or moderate sea. (Fig 1.2) (2) *Calms and light winds.* A flat calm means turning on the motor, drifting and waiting for wind or anchoring if there is a contrary current. As for light winds, these are surely the conditions when most people want to enjoy their sailing. The requirements are ample sail area including one or two good light weather sails and an efficient sail plan (see Chapter 5). Owners of low performance boats are sometimes heard to say 'she really gets going when the wind is force 5 or more.' What is the use of that? We all get going then. It is much better to make effective passages in enjoyable light weather. (3) *Sail changing or carrying the wrong sails.* If the

1.6 Sail changes are great time consumers.

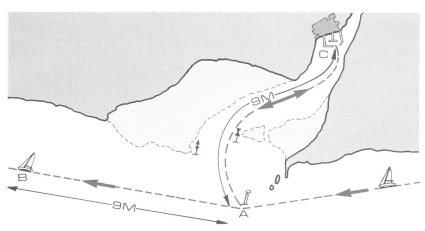

Fig. 1.3 A simple typical diversion into harbour. Rather than sail to B and onward, calling into port means three times the distance sailed: that is 18 miles A to C and back for the yacht harbour plus the 9 miles to B.

sail is not changed then it is wrong and speed is lost, but in my experience sail changing is a great time waster. This applies especially without a large racing crew, or when short handed. (Some solutions to this are in Chapter 4) (P 1.6). I sailed one long two-handed race in a yacht with a roller staysail, but otherwise conventional headsails (genoas and yankees) which had to be changed and ordinary reefing mainsail. We had a rival of equal size with roller headsail and 'in-the-mast' mainsail. When the wind was steady our rival lost out to us, but when the wind was up and down with much 'gear changing' required, he had the advantage. (4) *Navigation errors and sailing more distance than warranted.* Getting the wrong side of a shifting wind or miscalculating a current or tidal stream are time wasters. Chapter 8 discusses navigation for the fast cruiser, especially tactics to avoid bafflement by wind, weather and current. Much of this concerns actually sailing less miles through the water to achieve the destination. (5) *Making harbour.* Harbours are not highway service areas, where you just pull off and stop! If putting in to port on passage, not only must the time spent there be added to the total, but the diversion from course to make port. Some yacht harbours may be a long way up estuaries, others involve a circuitous approach. (Fig 1.3). Sometimes when the going is rough, there is a temptation to divert to a harbour. By the time you are there the weather has eased and keeping going offshore would have saved all that time.

These five factors apply to all types and sizes of yacht. Ways of overcoming them, when the skipper wants to do so, are discussed in later pages of this book. All boats however do not have the same potential: size and type determine speed before even setting out for a cruise.

Type of sailing yacht
Average and maximum speeds by size have been indicated above on the assumption that the yacht is a moderate fast cruiser or habitable ocean racer. *Size* is often determined by the funds available to the owner, but even this is not the whole story as a quiz of experienced cruising men conducted by an international cruising body showed. For long distance cruising, without cost being a factor, the percentage choices were as follows.

Under 23 ft LOA (7 m) Nil
23 ft to 29 ft (7 m to 8.8 m) 1 per cent
29 ft to 40 ft (8.8 m to 12.2 m) 58 per cent
Above 40 ft (12.2 m) 41 per cent
Unfortunately this survey did not sub divide above 40 ft (12.2 m), but one suspects that the percentage would have been small above about 55 ft (16.8 m) for obvious reasons of handling, finding crew and using small harbours.

As for *types* , these are legion and a matter of personal choice. New production boats appear from year to year and the author would not like to make any recommendation, other than the owner should choose a yacht to suit the kind of use to which she will be put and the waters in which she will sail. For instance a boat of an offshore one-design class that is present and raced regularly at his home port, but is not quite what is required for cruising, may be worth having because it can be raced locally. In another place it may be necessary to have a yacht that is

1.7 The latest racing yachts may be fast, but are often unsuitable for cruising.

strong enough to take the ground each tide, because of the local mooring situation.

When choosing a boat there are often certain types that stand out clearly and among these are the following. (1) The *modern racing yacht* has already been mentioned in the introduction as having become largely unsuitable for cruising (P 1.7). This is a sad development with various causes including the intensity of competition, especially international, following the adoption of an international rule in 1970 by all ocean racing countries. The authorities have done their best to grapple with the problem, but have failed to produce the 'dual purpose boat'. New materials and techniques have come just too fast for effective control, so one sees for instance the use of the 'blooper' sail. This is an expensive extra running sail which only adds a fraction of a knot (sometimes it slows a boat down!), but is 'free' area in terms of rating rules. It is certainly not free to buy! The rig of the early 80s, especially on boats less than 40 ft (12.2 m) is usually fractional, which implies a large mainsail, thin mast section and multiplicity of rigging including running backstays. (P 1.8). Decks have become virtually platforms for crew to run about on with only a foot well for the helmsman and no shelter. Keels have become very short (though this is not necessarily a poor feature; see below) and rudders are controlled by huge tillers in sizable boats to save the weight of a wheel mechanism. Recently sails may be made of materials totally unsuitable for handling when cruising, needing to be rolled in special bags or prone to sudden splitting. These faults may be acceptable when racing if the material is 'faster'. (2) An *older offshore racer* may well make a good fast cruiser. She was probably built before about 1976. The accommodation is fit for cruising with a usable cockpit and a masthead rig. (P 1.9). (3) The *production cruiser racer* or fast cruiser is an ideal basis for fast cruising and there are plenty of classes to choose from. However concept is not always the same as execution and any particular boat

1.9 *An older offshore racer is likely to be more desirable for cruising.*

1.8 A complexity of running backstays.

Fig. 1.4 *A separate keel and rudder does not mean necessarily a short keel. Here is the 'compromise profile' of the modern cruiser.*

should have construction for fast sailing (Chapter 2), be suitably equipped on deck (Chapter 3) and have accommodation for fast cruising and not just for use in the yacht marina (Chapter 10). The yacht may also need to have qualities or specification making it suitable for occasional racing (Chapter 5), short or single-handed sailing (Chapter 9) and heavy weather and emergencies (Chapters 6 and 7). The rig will almost certainly be a masthead sloop with perhaps an additional mast (a mizzen) if over 50 ft (15.2 m); profile would be fin keel and separate rudder, with or without skeg. (4) The *heavy displacement cruiser* may be the choice of some, its advantages being in extensive accommodation and a hull particularly suitable for rough use in, for instance, primitive harbours and grounding. Modern methods of construction mean that weight is not necessary for strength. Features such as heavy gauge rigging and a heavier section mast add to

cost. The keel may be a 'long' one with the rudder attached at its after end. There is also a compromise profile (Fig 1.4) where the keel is a partial fin and the rudder is on an elongated skeg. (5) The *motor sailer* may certainly sail, but the drag caused by deck structures in the air and below the water line for motoring, including a three bladed propeller (they cause immense drag), put the type out as a fast cruiser (in the sailing sense that we use it here) (P 1.10). She may be a handsome enough vessel, but her main requirement is performance and safety under power. The sails are for steadying, silent travelling, especially with a quartering breeze, and for fun. Many of the lessons in this book can apply, but the motor(s) and their supporting equipment must have

priority. (6) One further type is a dream for some and a most practical reality for others: that is the *one-off* or *custom* designed and built boat. To the novice almost any boat looks appealing, but to the experienced sailor no single boat seems to suit him. The custom boat is the answer, but be warned it is time consuming and expensive. A common compromise is a production hull with custom rig and interior: this could be a logical plan for the fast cruiser. The chosen designer will usually supervise the building and he is the key to executing the owner's needs. He does this by supplying detailed drawing to the builder and these are far from being just lines, layout and rig. (Fig 1.5). There are bound to be amendments and changes to the design as work proceeds; this is the advantage of custom building. The owner sees some building going ahead, but it is not quite as he envisaged it, so it is taken down and altered. Such changes increase the

cost and among all the other agreements that will have been drawn up beforehand are progress payments, insurance while building, acceptance trials and final payment, changes in costs of basic wages and materials; the procedure for pricing and charging such amendments must be clear to all parties. The custom boat is for those requiring special features, a particular standard of workmanship, or unable to find anything they want on the existing market.

Elements in design

Apart from classifying a boat as one general type or another, when choosing or assessing her, there are more specific guides in the form of the dimensions. When I am presented with a new design, I immediately want to know certain figures and these figures give me an instant idea of the capability and comparison with other yachts of the same size. *Length overall* is basic (LOA) and a

starting point. Then comes *load waterline* (LWL), *beam* and *displacement*. Then there is *sail area, draft* and *ballast keel*. An immediate difficulty is that different criteria are sometimes used for these dimensions; so look out for the following.

LOA should be the hull and all its main appendages, but no pulpits and bathing ladders. LWL can in practice vary with the load in the yacht and designed LWL may not work out: have you ever measured yours? It is not easy. (Fig 1.6). *Beam* varies at different points along the length of the boat, but here 'beam' conventionally means the maximum beam wherever found. *Displacement* is a tricky one. The designer gives a figure (or the manufacturer for a production yacht), but is it the actual displacement? How do you tell except by weighing the boat, which is seldom if ever done. It seems you have to accept the given figure unless it is observably way adrift. Sail areas are measured in different ways. For

17

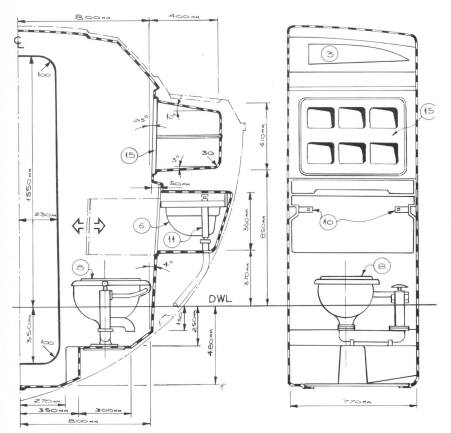

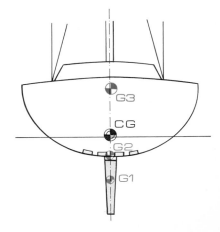

Fig 1.6 Length overall (LOA) and load waterline line (LWL) are absolutely basic dimensions to any yacht.

Fig 1.7 G1 is external ballast and its centre of gravity, G2 is internal ballast, G3 is the centre of gravity of all the hull and rig structure without ballast. 'Ballast ratio' indicates the proportion of G1 + G2 to the whole vessel (G1 + G2 + G3). The better the ballast ratio, the lower is CG (the centre of gravity of the whole vessel) but it can only be an indication owing to positioning of the ballast and the common lack of data on actual weights.

Fig. 1.5 List of drawings required for a 'one-off' design (below) and a typical detail (above) from one of them. A number of these drawings will consist of more than one sheet.

Lines, and offsets	Chainplates, stemhead and backstay
General arrangement (layout)	Rudder, steering gear, skeg and propeller
Deck plan and topsides and deck profile	bracket (strut)
Sail plan (with confirmation plan by	Joinery sections
sailmaker)	Joinery and internal furniture detail
Spar details (in conjunction with mast	Keel drawing and keel offsets
manufacturer)	Machinery, plumbing and electrical layouts
Construction profile	Supporting the drawings will be a complete
Construction section	set of written specifications
Construction detail drawings	

a sloop the mainsail could be half foot times luff (ignore the roach area) plus the area of the foretriangle (half height of mast times forward edge of mast to where forestay intersects deck). Some builders may quote the 'working jib', other the biggest sails and so on. *Ballast* is the weight of the lead keel, which should be known accurately plus internal ballast, if any. There is no reason why this should not be accurately known. With this figure and the displacement, the 'ballast ratio' will be known (Fig 1.7).

Fins and rudders

Once all yachts had long keels, some keels just not being quite so long as others. Now for the cruiser there is a choice of profile varying from the modern offshore racer hull with fin attached to a concave hull or traditional long keel with rudder attached. (Fig. 1.8) The profile is not the only story because the extreme fin invariably goes with light displacement. This fin has developed for two reasons. One is that the rating rule in racing has called for measurement at points some way out from the centreline, so that designers draw the section horizontally in from those points (Fig 1.9); the other reason is that modern building materials have enabled keels to be made thin and hull shapes to turn sharp corners.

Long keel versus short keel: what is the answer? The fact is that like so many aspects of sailing yacht design, opinions are divided. (That is part of the fun). The advocates of the long keel (and of course there are intermediate design positions which will temper arguments on both sides) cite its ability to take the ground, including alongside a wall, its tracking qualities (keeping going in a straight

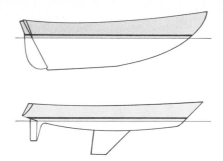

Fig. 1.8 Examples of profiles of both extremes of sailing yacht: very long keel with rudder attached and minumum keel area IOR racer.

line at sea without constant correction), possibly strength, ability to heave-to and the shape will be one of high displacement and therefore ample space below decks. Some may say that the long keel is 'healthy' or 'more seaworthy', but really these terms mean little without further explanation.

Long keel yachts have certainly come through bad weather, but then so have fin keeled vessels. One com-

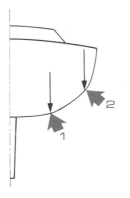

Fig 1.9 How the IOR measurement turning points have encouraged a certain hull profile with the hull meeting the fin keel horizontally.

plaint against the fin keel is that boats with it are prone to broach, but what is usually means here is the behaviour of racing yachts under spinnaker, when the cause is carrying excessive sail in strong winds and not the shape of the hull. The Dutch yacht designer E.G. Van de Stadt was producing boats with short keels and rudders separated thirty-five years ago; some were quite extreme with narrow fins. The record of his boats of all sizes and on voyages long and short and over many years has proved the short keel. The general trend to the separate keel and rudder did not occur until the mid sixties when the Cal 40 came in America (designed by Bill Lapworth) and other American designs succeeded in Europe such as *Rabbit* (designed by Dick Carter) and *Roundabout* (designed by Sparkman and Stephens). A number of years before then, John Illingworth had introduced several small ocean racing yachts with separate fins and rudders, but he told the author years later that other yachtsmen who wanted his designs would not accept anything so radical. The reason that the configuration was not adopted earlier

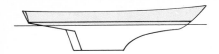

Fig 1.10 Short keel with rudder attached: an intermediate development in the 60s. With the rudder well forward steering was difficult.

(say the mid-50s), was that the fin keel designs were in general not, in the eyes of the then potential owners, markedly successful in racing. It was only when designers such as Carter, Lapworth and Stephens found the right hull form to make fin keel boats rate well and sail (very) fast, that the profile become general for racing.

Since then hundreds and hundreds of boats which never race have been built with the profile. There are boats with fin keels that are well designed and there are boats with fin keels that are poorly designed. One owner of a small (26.3 ft, 8 m) production sloop with fin keel and separate spade rudder who crossed the Atlantic (NW Europe – Portugal – Canaries – Bequia, West Indies) in the winter of 1982 has said of a severe gale 'We concluded that our light displacement was one reason why we had not suffered damage; when the force of the waves hit us, we gave and went with them instead of resisting. I must admit I was worried with the balanced hung rudder without a supporting skeg, but no damage was sustained. One large heavy displacement double ender crossing at the same time not only broke her pintles hove-to (presumably making a stern board), but the transom hung rudder then twisted right around and knocked the blades

off the propeller, just as the owner started the engine to help keep her nose up.' (see also Chapter 6).

The short fin keel means logically a separate *rudder*. At least it soon did in the mid-sixties, as keels became shorter and rudders attached to them became further and further forward. The result was that such boats became unmanageable in bad conditions. (Fig 1.10). I remember one of the last of these designs in which a dagger board was placed in the centre under the stern to try and help matters. A year or two later all new racing boats and indeed fast cruisers, were able, at last, to reduce the unnecessary wetted surface of the keel by cutting more away from it regardless of the rudder position, the latter being tucked away aft where (as some had all along known) its turning in the water has most effect on its leverage on the hull.

The question then arises whether or not a rudder skeg is desirable. Again conservatism would seem to favour a skeg. Hydrodynamic tests in smooth water have shown that a spade rudder with no skeg (P 1.11) at 15 degrees of turn delivered full turning power: this was 17 per cent more than a rudder with skeg of comparable size on a sister ship when turned to 20 degrees, which was maximum leverage. Over all turning angles the spade rudder gave higher

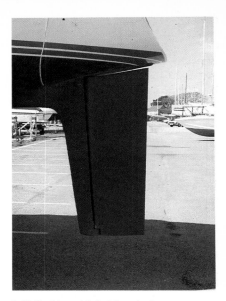

1.12 Rudder with full length skeg.

turning power. The drag on the skeg hung configuration was also greater. This is not however the whole story as strength is a major consideration. Support for the rudder along its length will be greater with a skeg (P 1.12), but I once sailed in a yacht where the skeg was so large that the vessel would barely respond to the helm (it had to be modified). A skeg part of the way down the rudder is a popular answer, so that a substantial proportion of the lower part of the blade is in 'free' water. It still has

1.11 Fully independent rudder.

an important difference from a spade rudder since its pivot point is on the forward edge, while the spade is swung from an axis about 20 per cent from its forward edge. Obviously the spade rudder stock must be very strong as immense dynamic forces occur where it emerges from the hull. The method of bearings within the hull to take the stock must be beyond reproach. In the event of damage to the rudder head or adjustments being made, it must not be possible for the whole stock and rudder to drop and sink. If a rudder is buoyant, it could still disappear in a seaway. (Typical construction might be a stainless steel stock and frame, glass reinforced plastics moulding (polyester or others) and foam filled.) Spade rudders can be inspected and repaired ashore, by being dropped down when the boat is held in slings or a crane. One further point about not having a skeg: several cases have been reported where yachts have foundered in very severe weather and it was thought that this might be due to the skeg splitting away from the hull and causing a disastrous leak, but nothing has been proved.

Performance by numerals

When comparing different yachts it is possible to quantify performance by using the available figures, even if these are sometimes of dubious origin. Three of the dimensions mentioned above will give useful ratios. These are the *displacement* (call it D), *the load waterline* (L) and *sail area* (S). The units used are pounds, feet and square feet; for metric units different constants and resulting figures will apply. In crude terms displacement slows you and length speeds you and the formula for com-

Boat 1. 20ft. LWL(L) Displacement 4000 pounds (D)
Sail area 252 square feet (SA)

The formulae are $D/L = \dfrac{D}{2240 \times (.01L)^3}$

$SA/D = \dfrac{SA}{(D/64)^{2/3}}$

$D/L = 252 \qquad SA/D = 16$

Boat 2. 40ft. LWL Displacement 36,124 pounds
Sail area 1093 square feet gives the same figures despite its different size.

Fig 1.11 Performance prediction for the cruiser by simple formulae.

paring these two is $D/2240 \times (.01L)^3$. Those with some mathematical knowledge will see that we have converted the pounds to tons and the length has been cubed for a direct comparison with weight/volume. We all know that Archimedes told us that the volume of water displaced by the floating body is directly comparable with the weight (displacement) of the body.

The other speed formula is $S/(D/64)^{2/3}$. This converts the displacement from pounds to cubic feet and then to square feet to compare to the sail area. Fig 1.11 shows the calculation of the ratios for two typical yachts. One has 20 ft LWL, displaces, so they say, 4000 lb and the sail area is 252 square feet; then there is a 40 footer of 36125 lb and 1093 square feet of sail. Rather than calculate each boat that comes along, Figs 1.12 and 1.13 show graphs which plot the ratios for different sizes of yacht. The terms 'heavy' and 'light' are relative and change over the years; modern materials have made it possible to build lighter boats than a few years back. One way of using the tables might be to take your previous or existing boat and see whether your next one is to be lighter/have more sail etc. Similarly one or two boats of admired proportions may be used as keys.

Though there are exceptions

Fig 1.12 Displacement-length ratios by the given formula from heavy to ultra-light.

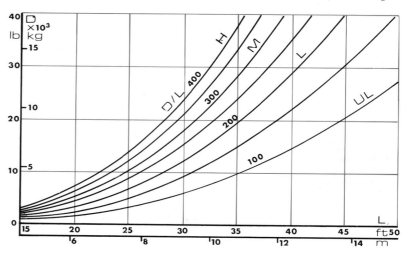

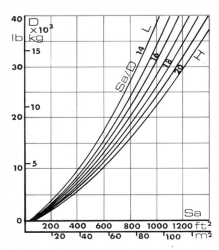

Fig 1.13 Sail area to displacement ratio figures from high sail area to low.

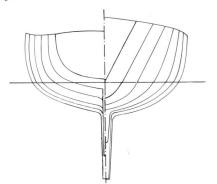

Fig 1.14 A section lines plan. This is the plan in a design which gives the greatest information about the hull characteristics.

(there always are in the inprecise world of yacht design, still an art despite the computers), the high sail area and high displacement boat will be faster in light weather because large displacement often goes with low wetted (frictional) surface. High displacement to length means less performance in fresh winds, since all that weight has to be pushed through the water each time the yacht moves her own (waterline) length. The high sail area to displacement does not help in fresh winds because by that time, sail is being reduced (reefed down). Similarly low sail area to displacement has no special significance in these fresh winds as the boat is at or near maximum speed. That leaves low displacement to length as the fresh wind flyer. Ultra light boats are for near-surfing down wind and not for fast cruising; their light weight is lost when much cruising gear is loaded. They also have other constructional and handling problems. So these figures and ratios, though representing only limited aspects of a boat and her performance, certainly apply to all.

Sections

Advertising and brochures for production boats and articles in magazines invariably show the profile of a vessel. This may well have the sail plan on it as well and it certainly gives an instant idea of the type of yacht. Yet there is a very important view of a boat which is much less frequently shown and that is the section. The 'section' is a view looking head-on or stern-on as it were, with a slice cut down at the point of maximum beam. Sometimes this is in the form of lines plans (Fig 1.14). To a reasonably practiced eye these lines give the best idea of all about

the character of the yacht: her general displacement, whether the keel is a fin, how thick or extensively faired into the hull (you cannot tell this from a profile), whether the bows are flat or full and the same with the stern and quarters. Freeboard is also made clear. It can be seen if the yacht is wide at the deck, or whether tumblesome actually reduces the width at the deck. Tumblehome is the turn of the topsides back into the hull towards the deck, which is not in fashion today as it reduces the width at the deck and accommodation space. Perhaps it really made wood planking easier to fashion.

A naval architect could draw out all of a boat's lines from a set of accurate sections. The only additional thing he would have to be told would be the length of the boat and the space between each section. If the sections are not available on paper, at least the mid (greatest beam) section would be better than nothing and give an indication of the sailing qualities of the hull. If no plans are shown, then the observer at a yard or boat show should sight the yacht from bow and stern to see this key shape. (P 1.13)

To some extent this shape reflects the displacement to length ratio discussed above, but this D to L figure depends on L which is not apparent from a sight of the section alone. Some sections are compared in Fig. 1.15 and the assumption is that these boats are all of equal length. Sections do not only tell you about speed, but have a direct influence on the following: accommodation, especially headroom and storage space (Fig 1.16), whether bilge water can be gathered in one place or if it will spread its dampness

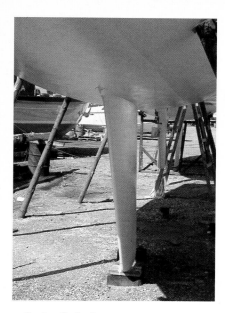

a. Racing fin keel.

b. Modern long keel.

d. Fin keel, but moderate displace ment.

c. Very heavy displacement section.

e. Compromise separate fin and long keel.

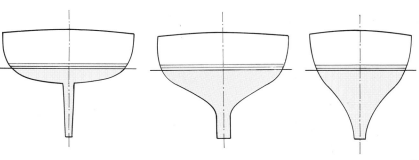

f. Oldies with keel attached rudders and propellers in apertures.

widely (though there are remedies that can be built in such as a sump trap), how much lift to windward is given by the keel, (in Fig 1.15 the left hand keel gives higher lift than the others) and 'form stability'. As is explained in all basic books or articles on yacht design, a 'saucer'-like section gives high initial stability, while a semi-circular section has no form stability at all depending on ballast

Fig 1.15 Differing yacht sections: light, medium and heavy displacement.

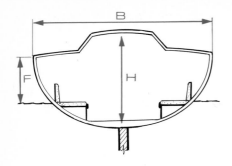

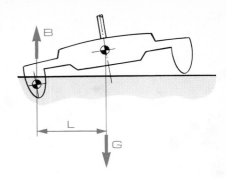

Fig 1.16 Accommodation amidships will largely depend on displacement, beam, freeboard and deck configuration including type of coachroof/cabin trunk.

Fig 1.17 Multihulls have immense stability and low angles of heel and so no need for speed-destroying ballast. Righting lever, L, between centre of gravity, G, and buoyancy, B, is large.

to keep upright. As the semi-circle is the least wetted surface, it is the 'fastest' at slow and moderate speeds. All yacht — and ship — design contains compromises of these facts.

Multihulls

There is another answer to this contradiction of stability. It breaks away from the laws of naval architecture applied to single ballasted hulls and produces great increases in speed across the whole speed range. This is the multihull, whose performance is indisputable. At first sight it should be the solution to fast cruising. The principles are well known. It relies wholly on form stability (Fig 1.17), thus enabling tons of lead ballast to be dispensed with, indeed all ballast. With such reduction in weight, but no less sail than a single hull of the same size, the multihull accelerates and sails much faster. The figures of some of the records given earlier bear this out.

Yet the snags are well known too and these must be the reason why multihulls remain in a small minority throughout the world for cruising. This is despite some epic voyages having been made and some cruising people sailing in multihulls happily year after year. The disadvantages

are: (1) Stability disappears very much earlier than on a single hulled yacht with ballast keel (Fig 1.18). While a ballasted yacht will usually come up from a knock-down (see Chapter 6), once the multihull has been tipped over she stays stable but inverted. All reports of multihull capsizes show that they are sudden and unpredictable and apply to the most skilled sailors. Devices such as masthead floats and instant sheet releases have not solved the problem. (2) The great beam makes entering harbour, finding moorings and berthing very difficult. Especially trimarans have no deck for relaxing or easy handling at close

quarters. (3) Weight is critical to performance and stability. For this reason long voyages in multihulls are invariably confined to very small crews. They are of course ideal for singlehanded and short handed races. (4) Construction can be difficult owing to stresses and strains at joints of hulls and beams, but designers and builders experienced in multihulls know how to cope with this. Space below and accommodation can work both ways and depends on the type. Broadly speak-

Fig. 1.18 The problem of multihulls: increasing loss of stability at 30 degrees and none after 90 degrees.

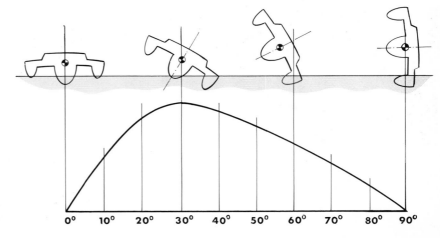

ing there are two concepts of multihull (P 1.14). There is the 'racing machine' with large sail area, slim hulled with very little room for those (few) aboard. Then there is the 'floating raft', usually a catamaran, with ample space between the floats and in each hull. Her sail area will be moderate for safety reasons and her speed markedly inferior to the multihull racer. She also shows no advantage in speed over the single hull. As a production boat she is sold on 'spacious accommodation' (such as cabins in separate hulls) and 'stays virtually upright'.

Against the cruising disadvantages given above, there are some secondary plus points. (1) If the multihull does capsize, she will not sink as a ballasted yacht would eventually, but remains afloat. A number of multihulls are equipped with escape hatches and emergency gear that can be used in the inverted state and there are records of crews existing like this for long periods. Provided the hull has positive buoyancy, collision damage and holing will not result in sinking; again, with exceptions, this does not apply to ballasted yachts, whose lead will take them rapidly to the bottom. (2) Shallow draft with no fin keel means that the multihull can be beached in suitable waters and weather. (3) Lack of initial heeling, mentioned above, is a physical pleasure for the crew, especially when cooking and navigating.

Multihulls for fast cruising can in theory be *catamarans, trimarans* or *proas*. The latter is hardly a cruising proposition. The *proa* has to be the same at bow and stern and have her mast amidships, or two masts equidistant from the centre! She needs rudders (retractable) both ends as well, because in order to tack or gybe, she has to stop and then set off with her single float to leeward. A proa has crossed the Atlantic, but the history of the configuration is mainly one of failure. Her speed advantage is that in only having one float she cuts drag. When the sole outrigger is to windward, the craft is called a Pacific proa.

Both the main central hull and the floats of *trimarans* are likely to have sections close to a semi-circle below the waterline, for reasons mentioned above. The centre hull is bound to be narrow by single hull yacht standards and deck space very restricted, making, for instance, sail handling difficult. Weight must be kept under control because if it does increase, due to extra crew, their gear, stores and cruising equipment in general, the whole speed advantage will decrease rapidly. She may also sink enough to make the cross arms to the

1.14 The cramped accommodation in one hull of a 60 ft. catamaran.

1.15 Catamaran with ample accommodation.

floats nearer to the water, so that they hit waves in certain conditions. Sinkage also means that both floats may be immersed in the water, though designed to have one floating and the other nearly clear and the ratio of float to hull buoyancy will be altered. All these possibilities are serious for a trimaran and show why she must remain at her designed displacement. Nevertheless it is a wonderful sensation when a moderate, fresh or even strong wind starts to move a tri and she sails at 10, 15, 20 or even more knots, making ordinary offshore sailing seem part of a past age. (P 1.2).

Catamarans were first on the offshore scene and have notched up more long distance cruises. They are also, as mentioned, available as production boats for more sedate cruising with a wide platform having preference over speed (P 1.15). Trimarans took over for racing in the 70s and the two-handed transatlantic race was won at 8.57 knots in 1981 and the single handed at 7.6 knots in 1984; both these were east to west against the prevailing winds. No single hulled yachts came anywhere near them in these events, though 'maxi-' single hulled ocean racers with big crews have attained these speeds over other courses. In the early 80s, big catamarans were becoming increasingly popular for short handed long distance racing. (P 1.16). One of the problems with the catamarans was the strength of the cross beams which are longer than on a tri. New materials and techniques are enabling these problems to be overcome. A cat needs two rudders, one on each hull and these have to be synchronized. It is possible to take the living accommodation away from the centre and

1.16 *Almost no living space on this racing cat.*

place some in each hull (if the yacht is large enough), though on a production cruising type facilities will be both there and in the centre as well.

It is not possible to generalize on the relative speed of cats and tris. There are just so many different designs: progress continues at breakneck speed compared with single hulls, that have been around for yachts for so much longer. In theory a trimaran is faster in light air as she can lift one hull and save wetted surface. In heavier winds, the catamaran lee hull is more able to support the heeling and displacement forces, while the tri float may be heavily immersed and the weather float causing windage. But these are theories and there are too many other variables.

If big catamarans do get more development in the years immediately ahead, it could be good for fast cruising. The racing and 'caravan' cats might be brought closer together to discover another breed of fast cruising yacht. But at present to cruise in a multihull is very much an individual decision.

2. Built for strength and speed

If multihulls are a way to reduce weight drastically, it is not a course which evidently appeals to the majority. The search is still on to cut down weight in the conventional single hulled yacht. Lightness is speed even with a lead keel being dragged around, for remember that the lead keel is only there to lower the centre of gravity of the whole vessel to give stiffness and therefore power under sail. If the weight of the hull, rig and rest of the structure is light, then the lead keel itself can be of less weight. Alternatively the centre of gravity will get closer and closer to the keel itself giving the boat great stiffness and righting ability, but to what extent is a matter for the designer.

The other side of the coin is that every unnecessary pound of weight slows the boat down both on and off the wind. Off the wind it is particularly disadvantageous, because

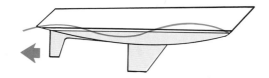

on the wind the weight is at least giving stiffness and therefore contributing to drive (Fig. 2.1). Off the wind the available sail area simply has to push the displacement value of the water aside each time the yacht sails her waterline − at least that is the basic way of looking at it. Weight of hull therefore means extra sail area which is costly in terms of sails and rig and more trouble to handle, or it means slower speed; once again it is loss of speed in light and moderate winds, the very time that you should be making fast passages in pleasant conditions.

Construction needs

Yet fast boats have a contradictory need: strength. Unlike day sailers or marina dwellers, the fast cruiser needs strength of hull, rig and fittings to sail fast, to sail reasonably long distances and to sail when the going gets heavy. A modern problem is that because many production sailing cruisers are used only for day sailing and gentle sorties from the marina, builders make some of them only strong enough for that. I do not blame them, for these kind of uses put them in a quandary: who will pay a higher price for strength which will never be tested? The builders do not actually say that this or that boat is 'weaker', but she is cheaper to purchase and there are clues to show that

she is not intended for serious passage making.

Back to fast cruising and the kind of strains which a boat has to undergo. Strangely boats are subject to many more recurrent strains than other objects that we usually handle. Houses are only tested to destruction in an earth tremor; cars suffer damage only on collision. But sailing yachts are under stress in ordinary and expected courses over the sea. If

2.1 Grounding is one reason for hull strength.

saving weight means paring down the amount of materials used, it is clear that danger ensues. For cruising, lightness cannot be achieved at the cost of structural integrity. Among the immediate causes for the need for strength are (1) Minor *knocks* and heavier *collisions*. Striking another yacht, gentle or hard, or coming against a quay or post harder than was intended should be able to be taken as part of normal cruising and not mean return to boatyard. Grounding comes into this category, even with some bumping up and down on rock, gravel and other hard bottom surfaces. (P 2.1) (2) *Rigidity*. If the hull flexes as the boat sails, then the rig cannot function effectively. Those expensive sails and spars will go out of shape and, more important, yield to the wind instead of making use of its power. For instance on a masthead rig, a backstay may be tightened up to make the forestay more rigid, (Fig 2.2) but no effect results because tightening the backstay has merely pulled up the stern. (3) *Pounding*. Depending on the shape of the bows some yachts pound heavily when sailing to windward in a seaway. The yacht seems to come down on a wave from time to time with a terrific bang that seems to shake everything aboard. Bow panels can flex if not properly stiff and damage can result to gear forward. I have experienced a ceramic toilet smashing, an anchor locker drain pipe severing and in the days of conventional wood construction, caulking being lost. A light hull can sometimes be felt 'wringing', as it crashes down. (4) *Integrity against heavy weather.* When seas start to come aboard in the form of heavy spray and then as a breaking wave top, then even as a breaking sea (Chapter 6), the hull and deckworks must withstand the tremendous forces imposed. You can feel some of this force if a sea sweeps the deck when you are standing on it and the water tries to push your legs away — it is an unpleasant reminder of the strength of the sea. (5) *Fastening and joints* are for ever under stress and must be carefully engineered: among examples are the motor fixings, including steps against vibration and the effects of it running when the boat is heeled, deck to hull joint, the mast step area, method of fastening the chain plates (which carry the tension of the shrouds) in or on the hull, the same for the forestay fixing and the backstay where it joins the hull at

or near the stern, the rudder itself and the way in which it affixes to the yacht.

Construction materials

Luckily boats are not the only vehicles in the modern world where lightness with strength is looked for: in recent years various man-made substances have become available for yachts from the aero-space industry. Cost, weight and strength and of course the ratios between these are what the designer works on when choosing what to put in a particular boat or production class of boat. As for strength, this has three aspects where hull construction is concerned. *Tensile* strength (in pounds per square inch/gms per cm^2) indicates how strong a material is when it is pulled apart. Parts of the hull are under tension as the rigging is set up and so, of course, is the rigging. The forestay has its tensile strength tested continuously. *Compressive* strength (in pounds per square inch/gms per cm^2) is the ability of the material to withstand a crushing force. The keel bolts testing the compressive strength of the hull (heavily reinforced and structured in such a vital area). As the yacht moves in a sea there is additional shock

loading on this compression strain; indeed shock loads are prevalent at all stress points around the yacht, for obvious reasons. Thus static stength is not enough in boat construction. *Stiffness* is the third measure of strength. It has been indicated above why this is important. Flexibility is the opposite quality and it may be useful in some parts of the boat, but not others. The measure of stiffness of a substance is its modulus of elasticity (pounds per square inch/ gms per cm^2). Fig 2.3 shows the comparison using these terms of strength between some common boatbuilding materials.

Glass reinforced plactics is the most common form of boatbuilding today. It has many variations and progress continues with new materials and new techniques. It is common knowledge that the material of which the hull is made started off as a *resin* and a *reinforcement*. Here are some of the resins. (1) *Polyester* is the most common and the lowest price, partly because it is relatively easy to work. It is heavier than some of the more exotic materials. It is, like most of the resins, a two part material: once a catalyst is added the polyester starts to cure. Mixing proportions,

Fig 2.2 Rigidity of hull is essential to withstand forces from the rig, especially if a tensioner, A, is used to tighten backstay and thus forestay. Both tend to pull hull against compression of mast heel.

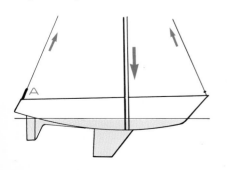

Fig 2.3

MATERIAL	WEIGHT	TENSILE STRENGTH	COMPRESSIVE STRENGTH	MODULES OF ELASTICITY
hard wood (modern techniques)	moderate	moderate	poor	fair
g.r.p	moderate	moderate	fair	high
aluminium	very light	high	high	high
steel	heavy	very high	very high	very high
ferro-cement	heavy	poor	fair	fair
kevlar	very light	very high	very high	very high

temperature and control are vital and yacht survey societies (eg American Bureau of Shipping and Lloyds Register of Shipping) for this reason check yard procedures in order to 'classify' yachts. This could be a useful safeguard since finished polyester may look the same whatever the quality. Polyester resins vary in their exact chemical content and manufacturers offer grades with specified qualities to builders. New techniques may demand close cooperation between builder and resin supplier to find the correct mix. (2) *Epoxy* resin is more flexible than polyester, it has a good adhesion, but is more expensive and a bit more difficult to work. It is therefore used as reinforcement, repairs and for bonding wood and metal to polyester (to which it adheres well). Epoxy is not only used with man-made reinforcement, but also with wood laminates with moulded wood systems for hulls (see below). (3) *Vinylester* is a light weight variation of polyester, in that

2.2 Raw materials of building in glass.

it has higher tensile and compressive strength. It is worth considering for a light weight version of a production hull using the same mould as is normal for polyester.

Reinforcements to go with the resins are more numerous. (1) *Glass* comes in the form of fibres or filaments (Glass fibre, Fiberglass, Fibreglas®) It is in rolls of fabric in varying weights. Three types are commonly used in boatbuilding: chopped strand mat, cloth and woven roving (P 2.2). Because of the varying properties of the weaves, all are used in different aspects of the boat. Woven roving and mat are used in the hull and structural members in varying combinations, often alternating, while cloth, being thinner and holding less resin tends to be used as sheathing or a finishing layer in a laminate. Even glass is not all of the same manufacture and *S-glass*, a typical aero-space product has some 35 per cent better tensile and compressive stengths and slightly better stiffness than ordinary extruded

2.3 Carbon fibre mat.

glass filaments (sometimes known as *E-glass*). S-glass is much more expensive, so is sometimes used for back up near keels, deck edges and so on.

(2) *Kevlar®* is a name widely known, partly because it is also used in sail making. It is a synthetic aramid fibre of low weight and high tensile strength. In combination with vinylester resin, it can be laid up over a rigid framework to give thin, light laminates with negligible stretch. For racing boats it can make a complete hull, or for others it can be used for extra strength and important structural members in combination with glass. (3) *Carbon Fibre,* (or graphite fibre) also from aero-space, has been round a long time, is very stiff, perhaps brittle in ordinary terms, with high compressive strength. It is more expensive than Kevlar and consists of long extruded graphite fibres of nearly pure carbon (P 2.3). It is used for back up in high stress areas. It is a prime example of the need for the correct use of exotic materials: rudders made of carbon fibre had numerous failures in 1979-80. One of its problems (or advantages if properly used) is that it is unidirectional with the fibres all running in one direction, in which direction it has almost all its strength. (4) *Sandwich* or *core* construction uses

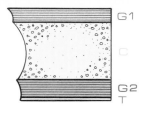

Fig 2.4 Typical core construction, for instance balsa or PVC foam (C). G1 is inner skin of GRP (or Kevlar etc.) About 15% of thickness, G2 is outer skin, about 20%, T is gel coat to give smooth waterproof finish.

several materials to stiffen hulls and decks and reduce weight. *End grain balsa* is the oldest to be used: small squares of this very light wood cut with the grain exposed. This is between GRP panels and is common for decks which inherently lack stiffness because they lack the compound curves of a sailing yacht hull. Balsa has been used a lot for one-off boats built on male moulds with a final layer of glass fibre covering the core and having to be faired up. More recently balsa is used in conventional female mould hulls, sometimes in the topsides with the lower part of the hull laid up in layers of glass fibre only. This gives lightness to the topside where it is needed. A core construction is good for insulation, but more liable to impact damage as the outer skin is thinner than conventional glass: the complete sandwich has high compressive stength and, as already indicated, high stiffness. (Fig. 2.4)

Lightweight *foam* cores are an alternative to balsa. These go under various trade names such as Airex®, plasticell®, which are PVC foams and Klegecell® which is a cross linked PVC- di-isocyanate mixture. More exotic foams still are appearing from the aero-space industry. Some are very light and stiff, but without high compression and tensile strength, but this makes them suitable for internal furniture of rac-

ing yachts and for some internal weight saving in cruisers. Others have high strength in all respects, but are currently very expensive, so perhaps used in limited parts of the hull only.

Traditional materials
There are still plenty of *wood* yachts sailing: for most people the need will be to know how to repair and maintain a boat of this substance rather than consider it for modern construction. There are still builders who will plank up a boat as has been done from earliest history (3000 B.C.) until about 1960, when plastics swept (almost) all before it. The ad-

vantage is aesthetic pleasure (P 2.4) and possibly easy repairs in primitive spots in the world, but, after that, cost, weight, strength, maintenance, even resale, are all against wooden boats. Cold moulding of wood veneers has continued for racing boats and this has been developed by using resorcinol glues (which are totally water and boil proof), so the difficulty of making tight curves in wood without numerous joints is overcome; more recently epoxy resins have been used to saturate wood veneers (in the WEST® system) which increases the compression strength of the wood without losing its tensile strength. It looks nice, is probably cheaper than the more exotic filament and foams, but wood must be a loser for the fast cruiser unless you love it and are prepared to pay for it. On many smart looking boats the only wood on the exterior consists of the tiller and hand rail along the coachroof

2.4 Modern wood construction.

(cabin trunk); perhaps some trim on it too! Inside is quite a different matter; for cabin furniture, bulkheads and cabin sole.

Metal boats have made many voyages and lasted a long time. The main problem is corrosion and the best way of overcoming this is to ensure meticulous construction and selection of metals, especially for equipment and fastenings. *Light alloy* (aluminum/aluminium alloys) was popular for racing yachts until the advent of newer plastics. Obviously they were built for strength, lightness and particularly rigidity. Despite special alloys and careful insulation, pitting and decay must be looked for if buying a used metal boat for fast cruising. Knocks can cause dents and major repairs will need a yard able to cut and weld alloy, which may be difficult to find and be expensive. It is all a long way from chemically inert plastics and easily cut and honed wood. By the way, 12-metre racing yachts are built of light alloy because of the construction rules of their class. (P 2.5)

Despite special marine *steel*, it is going to be heavy, yet once welded forms an extremely strong structure against both harbour wear and heavy weather. Bernard Moitessier, who sailed round the world one and a half times without stopping and then thousands of miles on other voyages, was knocked down ten times and says that he suffered no lasting damage because of the massive steel hull of his 34.5 ft (10.5 m) yacht *Joshua*. But he never pretended she was light in weight.

For many years a few boat yards, but many amateur builders, have made yacht hulls from *ferro-cement*. A framework of steel rods and then mesh is formed over the shaped frames of the hull. Up to eight layers of mesh are wrapped in position and then cement of fine consistency im-

2.5 Aluminium construction.

pregnates the structure, layer after layer of it. The steel and the cement are the cheapest of all the building methods reviewed in this chapter. Although a ferro-cement ocean racer once won the Sydney to Hobart race, the material is potentially heavy, nor does it lend itself to awkward bends and shapes. It is not therefore for building a fast cruiser, but it has proved suitable for amateur construction and maintenance. If the hull takes a hard knock, it may pulverize locally, but is unlikely to fracture or split, or even dent, as in other kinds of surface.

A quick survey
When considering a production fast cruiser or the purchase of a used boat, there are some useful checks that can be made by the potential owner. These are long before deciding to buy or having a professional survey. (Fig 2.5). These points apply to reinforced plastics only. (1) Hull fairness. Sight along the topsides and check for bulges at bulkheads and structural members. Unfairness does not necessarily mean lack of strength, but it implies lack of rigidity or bad finishing. (2) Roving print-through. You may see this as well, so why buy a bad finish?

(3) Hull-deck connections. On new boats, the builder may well specify how this is done (unless he is not proud of it). Check for any bolting or other repairs. (4) Chainplates. How exactly are the shrouds finally connected to the hull? These should be massively locked into the plastics hull structure. See if there are signs of stress in this area. There should be complete watertightness where the chain plates pass through the deck. (5) Bulkheads and cabin furniture. The former should be filleted into the hull and able to withstand unfair

Fig 2.5 A quick survey.

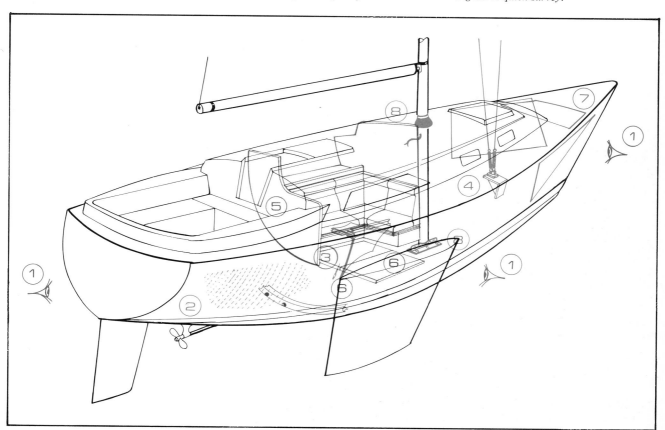

stress below such as crew crashing against them from any direction. (6) Bilge. All parts must be accessible, able to be pumped out (preferably at an ordinary angle of heel). Limber holes must allow drainage. Cabin sole boards must lift easily, not be swollen by damp. (7) Deckhead. The surface overhead if covered in fabric should be tightly bonded, or alternatively stand off so that there is adequate ventilation to prevent condensation and mildew. It must be possible to reach fastenings securing deck fittings without undue 'rebuilding the boat'. (8) Masthead partners and step. If the mast is stepped below, is the area where it passed through the deck completely waterproof and is the mast step arranged to spread the great load of the spar? If the mast is deck stepped there must be a massive support or bulkhead immediately below it and electric wiring which emerges from the mast above deck must connect inside the yacht and not on deck.

Though these are only a few points, if many of them are not right, it is likely that the boat has not been built (if new) or maintained (if used) in a state suitable for fast cruising.

3. Equipment above deck

Much of the pleasure of fast cruising comes from operating efficient gear which gets the best out of the boat. Too many indifferently sailed cruisers have equipment on deck and in the rig, which is there because it has always been there and it slows the boat, because it takes time to use or is just a factor in making the boat a little slower. Perhaps the previous owner had it like that or it has become out of date, or — I regret to say — the builder could have equipped the boat more thoughtfully. Even on a new boat, the gear should not be left as it is, but improved for the pleasure of fast cruising. The fact is that many standard cruisers are not properly equipped because the builders have to offer them as 'standardized' to keep the price down to

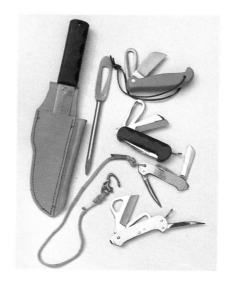

3.1 An essential equipment to be carried by each crew member.

that of competitors. This really is a major factor when choosing a yacht.

Equipment qualities

First of all comes good design and in this it is only possible to judge each piece of gear on its merits: access, does the job quickly, does not break down owing to chafe and so on. The common qualities if a little obvious are (a) *strength,* but often this means strongly secured as with through-bolt stanchions, handholds, cleats and tracks; (b) *lightness,* because you cannot just keep adding weight and expecting the yacht to go as fast. Throw out clever but heavy fittings; (c) *low windage* is essential otherwise there is all that wind resistance of big cowls, pram hoods, dodgers, various booms and poles lashed in the shrouds — and do you really need all those flag halyards, so seldom used?

There is one other quality for equipment and that is personal usefulness. This is as good a point as any to mention that each member of the crew should have efficient personal equipment which he carries. Number one is a sailor's knife (P 3.1) and some form of spike which may be in the knife. Some tape and twine in his pocket will not go amiss and a small adjustable spanner (= wrench) will mean instant action rather than having to make for the yacht's tool kit.

Mooring and anchoring

Arrangements for mooring and anchoring need to be effective, but they will not help the yacht to go any faster on passage. Offshore racers have no cleats and will be seen moored in marinas with lines made fast to other fittings. (P 3.2) The 76 ft (23.2 m) *Flyer* (Holland) winner of the 1981–82 round the world race, had no stemhead fitting or special anchoring arrangements as her aim was to stop only at three ports *en route*. Anchors on the stem head fitting (P 3.3) are bad for speed and can

3.2 *Mooring cleats are considered unnecessary in ocean racers.*

even be dangerous. Lashed on deck they are not much better; in a special deck well they are still in a position which is bad for stiffness and bad for pitching (P 3.4). For fast cruising the anchors (there must be at least two of them), should be lashed down below. If the focsle has to be used, then the anchors should be aft within it, secured perhaps to the after bulkhead in the fo'c'sle. Holes can be drilled through it to take lashings. Unlike ocean racers there can be some compromise on cleats. These can be very light weight (alloy), but strongly secured. Two forward and two aft will fill most functions. Devices to stop them fouling lines at sea are advisable (Fig 3.1). If there is no stemhead fitting for anchor cable or rode and conditions are heavy, try using a snatch block (Fig 3.2) and the ordinary port or starboard fairlead. Such fairleads are very useful, but aft they can be dispensed

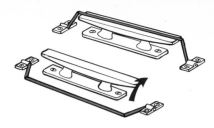

Fig. 3.1 *A simple hinged wire will stop a cleat fouling running lines when sailing.*

Fig 3.2 *Without a heavy stem head fitting, it is sometimes difficult to haul up an anchor warp: a big snatch block ready to rig on the bow cleat can help.*

3.3 *An anchor permanently on the stemhead.*

3.4 *Special deck well for anchor is now common.*

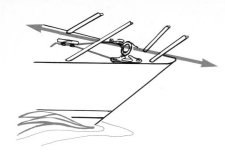

Fig 3.3 For a heavy tow rope a large steel ring secured forward will guide the tow line back to the mast to which it is secured.

with in favour of big cleats which can also be used when sailing for sheets and other running gear. If much anchoring is envisaged, a proper anchor lead over the stem is recommended. In the Fastnet '79, lifeboatmen criticized yachts for not having suitable fairleads to pass a heavy tow rope and use for a long distance tow. It is therefore useful having a ring of about 3½ in (80mm) diameter which can be rigged forward and then a tow can be passed through it. (Fig 3.3).

Steering and cockpit area
The cockpit is from where the crew

3.5 Tillers are in fashion on large racing boats.

enjoy their sailing and many are the designs and ideas for it. The most important element is that the helmsman must be able to see the compass. If there is a wheel this is usually not difficult as the compass will be on a binnacle which may also be used for engine control, wheel mounting and lock and other instruments. In the USA most yachts of 32 ft (9.7 m) and upwards have a wheel, but in Europe tillers are quite common up to 40 ft (12.2 m). There is currently a tendency to get rid of wheel steering on racing boats up to even larger sizes on grounds of weight and accurate steering. (P 3.5). The compass must be near enough for the helmsman to read it; it must be on a level so that he is looking forward (at the seas and other vessels) and not obscured by the crew (Fig 3.4). The last is often the most difficult to achieve. Twin compasses in the after end of the coachroof should be towards the centre line, so crew can sit back clear of them (Fig 3.5).

To steer the boat effectively and therefore quickly, the helmsman must be comfortable for hour after hour. This is fairly easily achieved with wheel steering using a seat aft of the wheel and sometimes shaped to enable the helmsman to sit to windward of leeward. With a tiller it is not so easy, mainly because as the boat heels the man on the helm needs to sit in quite different positions. One approach is to ensure that the coaming section has seating positions for the various angles of heel. Once the helmsman is sitting well out against the life-lines, then these too need to be made comfortable: wrap foam rubber around them for his back, (P 3.6). Another system is straps aft, additional and in extension of the wire life-lines. The tiller must have

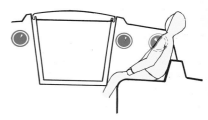

Fig 3.4 and 3.5 With wheel steering siting a compass is relatively easy: it is usually on a pedestal or structure just ahead of the wheel on the centreline. Siting a steering compass or compasses for the tiller steered yacht is sometimes difficult (3.4) and must be carefully planned for each different cockpit layout. The helmsman needs to look generally forward (A) yet the crew (B) can easily obscure a compass position. He cannot keep looking down, if the compass (C) is close below him. If it is on a coachroof at eye level (D), it may be too far away.

If bulkhead compasses are used (3.5) either side of the companionway, they should be close to it, otherwise crewmembers sitting in the cockpit will obscure it.

Fig 3.6 *Have a tiller designed to be as comfortable as possible — there is no need to stick to a traditional varnished wood stick. Here are shown both, a fixed and hinged extension.*

3.7 *A 'centre' cockpit with cabin aft of it.*

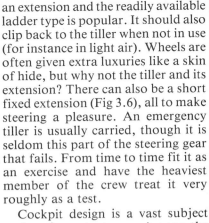

an extension and the readily available ladder type is popular. It should also clip back to the tiller when not in use (for instance in light air). Wheels are often given extra luxuries like a skin of hide, but why not the tiller and its extension? There can also be a short fixed extension (Fig 3.6), all to make steering a pleasure. An emergency tiller is usually carried, though it is seldom this part of the steering gear that fails. From time to time fit it as an exercise and have the heaviest member of the crew treat it very roughly as a test.

Cockpit design is a vast subject and an important one. Among the many variations there are three basic types for a sail boat: centre, separated (by large bridge deck, for instance) (P 3.7), or virtually adjoining saloon (P 3.8). For fast cruising only a couple of aspects can be con-

3.8 *Bridge decks at two levels separate cockpit and companionway*

3.9 *An opening aft cockpit cannot trap water.*

3.6 *For the helmsman to lean against the rail.*

sidered. First quick drainage in the event of filling and this is dealt with in Chapter 7. An open transom (P 3.9) gets rid of the water quickly, but has some cruising inconvenience (harbour use). This is the exact opposite of the centre cockpit, which for all its advantages is the most dangerous if filled by a sea, letting water into cabins fore and aft. Second, how many crew are going to use the cockpit at the same time? In the ocean racer with only a foot well the crew are all out on deck; so can they be in a cruiser in fine weather (but there must be deck space!). On passage in poor weather some are below so only 40 per cent of the crew needs the cockpit. Again wheel steering gives more space for crew seating, but with a tiller seating must be sacrificed where the stick sweeps the area. A grating looks smart, but it is heavy and can float up in a filled cockpit to jam gear. You can forget it. But the cockpit sole should be non-slip.

Being able to see the instruments is much the same problem as the compass. They are expensive so extra money spent on siting is worth it. Over the main hatch is common enough and practical except when some one is coming through it. (No one should stand there). An alternative is specially made mountings, which like the compass may need duplicating.

Mainsheet arrangements are important. There are now well developed arrangements for racing boats which are very much of application to fast cruisers. (P 3.10). Cruising yachts are often seen sailing on the wind with the mainsheet insufficiently hardened in: these devices will ensure that the sheet can be really tight and also released under control.

Mainhatch

Mainhatches are now well developed to be watertight and provide easy access below. On larger yachts there is usually a bridge deck or portion of deck to cross from the cockpit before descending into the hatch. This in turn slides into a moulded box, so no

water can run into the hatchway from forward. (P 3.11). Ledge baffles inside the hatch complete the job. On smaller yachts there is either a bridge deck within the cockpit, or the hatchway opens straight into the saloon. The latter is unsatisfactory, but if in a small yacht it is unavoidable, there must be strong bolts to hold lower boards in position, so water cannot flow from a filled cockpit to the accommodation. A small but essential item is a well secured gum rubber hatch stop at each after corner of the hatch. It acts like a hammer when being shut so must be brought up short; if such a stop did sheer, the crew could pull the hatch clean off in an emergency (the author once narrowly escaped such a situation).

Once the weather deteriorates washboards should be inserted. I do not like the practice of leaving them

3.10 A powerful mainsheet arrangement is essential.

3.11 A conventional efficient main hatch and box and with washboard safety latch.

out in gale conditions. If there is proper ventilation, there should not be any need to leave them out for the crew to breathe. If the cabin entrance tapers, then it only needs a board to rise an inch or so and it can fall out: (see Chapter 7) vertical entrances are preferable for this reason. In any case they should be secured by a lanyard, so they can never be lost and any fast cruiser must have a device between top washboard and hatch, (as explained in Chapter 7) so that both are locked in position when desired, but can always be opened from both below and from on deck.

Other hatches

These pose less problems, because at sea they are frequently permanently secured. There are now patent hatches of many sizes from various manufacturers. These vary from the excellent to the downright dangerous. A number come somewhere between these extremes! The best have the following qualities (P 3.12) (a) a system to raise the hatch partly so that *it cannot close* on someones head or fingers; (b) *hinges facing forward,* then a heavy sea cannot force open a hatch which has been inadvertently left not fully closed; (c) opening from *both inside and out,* and though it must be lockable for security, it must never be locked when persons are on board as it is a means of escape (at least one hatch of recent design security locks from the inside, so it is impossible to be locked in – only locked out!); (d) the hatch must *not be able to* slam down and *lock itself* automatically, as persons have been trapped like this, especially in lazarette and cockpit hatches, even when the boat is laid up in the back of a shed! (e) *the structure* should be raised slightly from the deck as flush designs are difficult to keep watertight; (f) *fabric covers* are a useful adjunct,

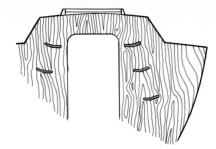

allowing the hatch to remain partly open yet still protected from spray when going to windward, or a flush storm cover helps withstand intense spray or water moving on the deck; (g) the corners and edges of the hatchway must be *non-fouling* to avoid torn clothing and sails (h) *access* up and down must be provided, for instance steps on a nearby bulkhead to obviate potential strains or injury. (Figs 3.7); (i) *translucent* hatches are practical, but should be tinted for privacy and 'safety walk' affixed to make them non-slip.

After many miles of sailing fast, I would advise on the subject of *cockpit lockers and hatches:* if possible, don't have 'em. The 'slower' the cruiser the bigger the cockpit lockers, while flush deck ocean racers know them not (P 3.13). The reason is watertight integrity. If there has to be a small one, perhaps

Fig 3.7 Access to a forehatch by means of steps on a bulkhead, sloped each side for when yacht is heeled. Without these, moving up and down can be difficult or dangerous.

Fig 3.8 Cockpit lockers should not drain into the yacht however 'watertight' they are designed. This shows a locker for gas cylinders; any escaped gas or water drain straight out above waterline. There is no connection to interior of yacht.

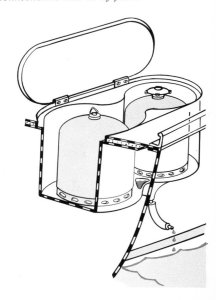

3.12 Non fouling fore hatch: note non slip strips.

3.13 This offshore racing cockpit has no lockers to cause leaks.

for a gas bottle or other specific piece of equipment, then the locker should be sealed from the rest of the accommodation and drain into the cockpit or over the side. (Fig 3.8).

Ventilation

Few standard production boats have adequate ventilation. This is because hatches can be opened in harbour, but at sea going to windward in spray or even in cold weather, they must be closed and then how do you breathe below? Stuffiness below is uncomfortable, nauseating and may force the crew to open a hatch for air just at the moment when a sea comes over. Lack of ventilation is bad for crew performance and therefore boat performance. Watertight vents that let in air but not water are nothing new (P 3.14) and readers of this book do not need to be told how they operate. What is needed is the will to install them. They are not difficult to add to an existing yacht. There should be two in the forward part of the main saloon and a model with an electric exhaust fan over the galley and the head. More than these depends on the size of the yacht. It is not necessary to ventilate the fo'c'sle, as it is difficult to repel the heavy water that may impinge on the

foredeck while the area below is not in use at sea. Open the forehatch in fine weather to air the place!

The engine room should have one or more blowers where fumes collect. Government regulations in various countries may well insist on the specifications for this. The fuel tank itself will have a vent, a thin pipe taken high up and usually outside the boat. Again there may be regulations or trade practice about this, but the author doubts if law makers know much about life on a fast sailing yacht. He has taken a fuel vent up inside the yacht, in way of the cockpit (Fig 3.9) where there is no

Fig 3.9 Fuel vent (diesel not gasoline) taken inside yacht cockpit coaming is preferable to salt water entering an exterior vent.

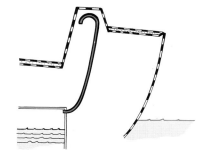

chance of ingress of sea water. He has found this satisfactory. (Which would you rather have after a knockdown, some diesel in the bilge or some sea water in the fuel? – you may need to choose.)

It must be possible to block off vents in an emergency. Standard cowls are often supplied with 'storm caps', but as well as these, some arrangement whereby vents can be blocked from below by screw, slider or bung (Fig 3.10) is more practical.

Fig 3.10 An example of watertight integrity throughout the boat. A screw-in bung can be used to shut off a Dorade vent from below, not from above which is undesirable in heavy weather.

It means less fiddling around on deck in heavy weather. Such bungs will be easily located from the emergency location list (Chapter 7).

Winches, stoppers and tackles
Stoppers (lever jammers) have come along in recent years, so they are now a practical proposition to reduce the number of winches and conventional cleats. That is to say they are positive and, most important, can be released under heavy load and with

control. Without this quality it is better to have a winch upon which a line can be eased away or a conventional cleat, which, of course, also makes it possible to control a halyard or other line under load. (P 3.15). If you see someone having to assault a stopper with the end of a winch handle, scrap it and replace it with a quality product. (Fig 3.11). The modern lever stopper has really replaced the famous Clamcleat except on the smallest cruisers.

Tackles may sound a bit old-fashioned, but have their uses for fast cruising. The most commonly used tackle will be the main boom preventer. This is invaluable when running in a seaway in light to moderate weather to stop the main boom swinging in board. (P 3.16). There should be a long lead off the tackle so it can be brought aft to a cleat near the mainsheet: then both sheet and preventer are used together, one having to be eased when the other is hardened. The same tackle can also be used as a main boom vang which stops the boom lifting when on a reach and prevents chafe. On the other hand, a fast cruiser must have a kicking strap, so this does the job anyway

3.15 Halyard or sheet stopper.

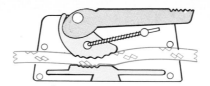

Fig 3.11 A good design of halyard/sheet stopper, where the pawl lifts off the rope so it can be released under load. It can be hauled in with the lever shut, usually by winch. When in position the line is merely cast off the winch which can be used for another line.

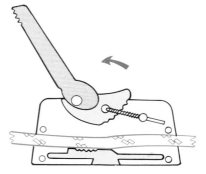

and the preventer only needs a mainly forward component. (In the USA the kicking strap (as used in Britain and Australia) is also called the vang; in Britain, it is only a vang when it goes to the rail.)

If there is a backstay on a hydraulic tensioner, (P 3.17) there should be a tackle made up with suitable end fittings, so it can immediately be substituted if the hydraulics fail. The vang and the backstay tackle will do for other jobs aboard the boat, where power needs to be applied.

Winches for yachts are now really first class, thanks entirely to their development for racing boats. They are powerful, attractive, making the control of lines under huge tensions easy and are fun to operate. Self-tailing winches have in the late seventies become a practical proposition and are a boon to the cruising man. The more short handed you are, the more

3.16 Main boom preventer: usually a snapped on line with ready tackle.

self-tailers, you need. There is little an ordinary winch will do that a self-tailer (ST) will not do and, as far as I can see, the only objection is cost, the ST being about 1.4 times the price of the exactly equivalent medium size winch. As for weight, in

3.17 A hydraulic tensioner should have an emergency back up tackle.

some ranges the STs are actually slightly lighter or about the same weight as a three speed; perhaps slightly heavier than a two-speed. We are talking about differences of less than 7 per cent. Anyway for each ST there is one less conventional cleat! The rule for fast cruising: *do not be underwinched.* There is always one size larger available and why not use it for ease of control and sheer pleasure? Many builders of standard yachts equip them with winches a size too small to cut down the initial price. A cruising yacht, which may at times be short handed or weakly crewed needs more powerful winches than a racer: in practice they should have the same, because the offshore racer has to do things quicker. So do we in the fast cruiser, when doing something like tacking up a narrow channel, or executing a tricky gybe. Adequate winching lessens possibilities of failure inside the mechanism.

The primary winches (that is the winches used for the main headsail sheets) should therefore be powerful top action, 2- or 3-speed of the best quality. (P 3.18). Charts of recommended sizes are available, but should be used as a guide only. (See *This is Down Wind Sailing* page 25). These primaries may be used for other jobs in addition to genoa sheeting, (and unwinding a furled jib) including breaking out an anchor, winching back to a mooring on a quay or elsewhere, or for hoisting a man in the bosun's chair. Do not put him on the halyard winch, that his halyard belongs to, but lead the halyard via a snatch block on the rail to the primary. Feels easier does it not? The ball bearing handle which you will have on these winches, also makes winding easier! Without such

bearings handles tend to clog and cannot be freed.

Secondary winches (intended for the spinnaker sheets) are best close by the primaries. The reason for this is that they can be brought into use to take the same loads, when changing a sheet or a riding turn has occurred on the primary. If they are on a different level (for instance on the coachroof) then such leads are difficult. Winches on the fast cruiser should be ruthlessly resited, if they do not obey the rules for correct positioning. These are (a) the incoming line should be at an angle to the vertical axis of the winch of between 95 and 125 degrees, otherwise riding turns will ensue; (b) maximum power must be applied by the winder and to do this he must be able to 'get above the handle' at least until the heel angle exceeds 25 degrees (after which most yachts should be brought back by sail reduction); (c) the handle must be clear when winding, of lifelines, low main boom, the main sheet in any position on its track and similar obstructions. The author had to have an 8-inch (20 mm) handle on one boat for certain winches, as the standard 10 inch (25 mm) as supplied struck the rail.

Positioning of other winches is not so critical. There may be winches for main and staysail and mizzen sheets, halyards of all kinds including headsails, spinnakers and main halyards (less powerful than headsail winch because of the angle of approach at the halyard block), mainsail reefing winch (jammers essential for taking in different reefs), spinnaker topping lift and foreguy. Jammers immediately come into their own when there are, for instance, duplicate genoa and spinnaker halyard. When both are under load, one is on the

3.18 *The primary winch is for the big headsail, but can play other roles.*

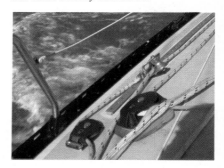

3.19 *Foot blocks are often essential, though not desirable. They can jam running lines and cause a heavy deck stress.*

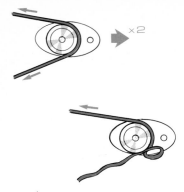

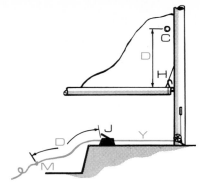

Fig 3.13 The main halyard (Y) is marked at M so that D on sheet equals D, distance between reef cringle (C) and reef hook, H. To reef, halyard is eased until M meets the stopper/jammer, (J). Then C can immediately be hooked on to H.

Fig 3.12 Foot blocks for genoa winches should be avoided if possible. They double the tension of the genoa sheet on the deck fitting, and when released can 'half-hitch' and jam in the block.

winch and the other in a jammer.

For sheet winches foot blocks (P 3.19) should be avoided where possible. They are a point of very high load (Fig 3.12) and they sometimes jam on a kink when the sheet is being run out. They may be necessary however to get the correct lead as in (a) above. Sometimes winches are mounted on a mast, especially for the main halyard and the main reefing cringle. For the fast cruiser this is undesirable because it causes weight higher than necessary, adds windage, puts the winch at an angle difficult to operate, see (b) above,

weakens the mast with extra fittings, causes potential electrolysis, causing maintenance and stowage problems when the mast is taken out ashore and is in a place where headsail sheets can foul. Both such winches could be well aft or elsewhere on deck where they are safer to use in heavy weather. For reefing, a jammer with the main halyard winch and a marked halyard enable just the right amount of halyard to be eased off, then jammed, for the luff reef cringle to be inserted in its jiffy reef hook. (Fig 3.13).

Modern winches are made of bronze (which is usually disguised by being chromed), light alloy (anodized) or stainless steel. Alloy and chromed bronze appear to be the same price: stainless is much more costly. The weight saving of alloy on bronze is one third. Stainless is frac-

tionally lighter than bronze. Alloy winches are now well developed and can be cruised without problems, but they do require more maintenance than bronze which can in comparison almost be neglected. My experience is that the smaller alloy winches tend to seize up if not frequently maintained.

Racing boats with active crews are forever stripping down and maintaining winches. On cruising boats this is not seen enough. It is an enjoyable task for an evening on board and I strongly recommend frequent inspection and taking down if necessary. The inside of winches tends to collect an amalgam of dried salt, dirt and grease (P 3.21). Manufacturers seem to supply new

3.21 Heavy grease in winch gears should be removed.

3.20 When stripping a winch guard against loss of components.

winches with excess grease in the works. The builder probably adds to the grease with sawdust! Maintenance therefore applies to new winches as well. Take the winch apart in accordance with the handbook, though often the way of stripping down it self evident. When removing the drum, shield below it with the hand, so that the needle bearings cannot slip over the side (P 3.20). Check no small components, such as pawl springs (Fig 3.14) are broken. The latest winches are designed to strip without being removed from the deck, but older models may have to be unbolted to reach all parts. On modern winches the tools needed are simple: screwdrivers, Allen keys, a small hammer and hardwood pad (to stop hammer damage) and a spanner if the winch has to be removed from the deck.

Wash out all parts with petrol, paraffin, gasoline or kerosene. Then replace them with a coating of light oil only. Some special winch grease may be very lightly smeared on flat parts or inside the drum, but *no grease* must get near the *pawls* or their *little springs*. For more routine maintenance, it is only necessary to remove the drum and bearings and

Fig 3.14 A pawl and spring from a winch. They must be kept clean and lightly oiled. Sometimes the pawl sticks (usually due to dirt, dried salt or over greasing) or the spring breaks. A pair hold each ratchet inside the winch and on such a tiny part, the handling of the yacht sometimes depends.

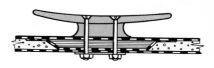

Fig 3.15 With sandwich core decks, the core must be cut away and infilled with glass and resin or other solid material, for any fittings to be secured.

clean. Spray light oil (e.g. WD 40) into the works (P 3.22), check pawls are clicking smoothly and replace the drum. Spares should be carried, but which? Obviously pawls and their springs, which can 'spring out' when reassembling; circlips and other small components as used in a particular model and any parts which have been found liable to fail. (P 7.3).

If such maintenance is not carried out it can only result in winch failure and perhaps even permanent damage. I read again the other day, that a rinse with fresh water will be helpful. I can only quote a winch maker (with whom I agree), that 'this will result in little more than a pair of rather damp feet'.

Tracks and sliders (cars)

Tracks are still the best way of providing variable positions for leads for headsails. Tracks may also be used for runners (rare), or for an inner forestay anchorage, which can then be tightened by forcing a slider forward (Fig 3.16). Like all other deck fittings, tracks must be through bolted and backed up by pads below deck depending on the deck material and its thickness. Sandwich decks (Fig 3.15) must be infilled to prevent crushing.

A common kind of track has alternate bolt holes and plunger holes and until recently this was acceptable and simple. The problem arises when it becomes necessary to move the car position, when the load prohibits it. Often the only way to do this is to let go the sheet completely, move the car and then winch the whole sheet in again — tedious! If there are plunger holes, by the way, they must be cut straight down and not chamfered (Fig 3.17), as this tends to allow the plunger of the car to ease out. But

3.22 Take apart, clean and spray with light oil.

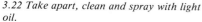

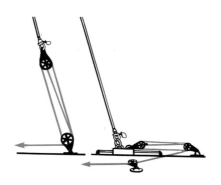

Fig. 3.16 Foot of an inner forestay (babystay), left shows simple block and tackle; on right a slider fulled forward by a tackle tightens the stay. In both cases a single line is taken aft.

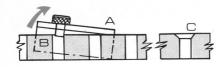

Fig 3.17 How a conventional car (A) with plunger, can be canted under load so that it jumps the track (B). On a genoa sheet, this means it suddenly moves aft several feet. Fairing the top makes things worse (C). The solution to this problem is at photo 3.23.

even when the plunger hole is cut straight, the car is likely to jump the track and slip aft under load. The more it does this, the more there is wear on plunger and plunger hole, so the trouble gets more frequent.

Therefore strongly recommended for fast cruisers is a track which does not use plungers to fix the car. What is needed is a slider, the position of which is held by a permanent tackle from forward (because the sheet pulls aft) and can be steadied by shock cord aft (P 3.23). For most rigs on fast cruising a single fore and aft track is enough for all sails. See Chapter 7 for remarks on the sheeting of the storm jib. For a cutter or double head rig, the staysail track will be forward and if inboard may

3.23 Note this genoa car is controlled by a line forward and shock cord aft and cannot jump out of position.

be on the coachroof. If the coachroof is of any width the main track will be close to it to get the genoa sheeted well inboard when close hauled. When reaching and requiring the genoa to be sheeted further outboard a second sheet can be taken to the ship's rail, or a barber hauler used. The mainsheet has been mentioned earlier in this chapter: it will run on a mainsheet track on which it imposes a strong upward tension. X-shaped tracks are available for this purpose with the mainsheet slider on multiple wheels. Heavy stoppers must be in place in case the slider slams across out of control, though the traveller tackles should control it at all times. It must be possible to haul the traveller up to windward under load, so a tackle which can be pulled up from the side deck should be installed. (P 3.24). It is a thorough nuisance, if a crew member has to scramble down into the cockpit and fight with the slider tackle each time it needs shifting.

Other deck features
Modern ocean racing rules only require a *toerail* (height at least 1 in/25 mm) forward of the mast. Cruisers should have them along the entire length of the rail (P 3.25). Your booted foot relies on it when on the lee deck and the modern light alloy types with plenty of holes drain quickly and have multiple securing

3.25 Useful conventional toe rail. Drains, takes shackles for fittings.

points for snatch blocks and similar temporary fittings. Permanently on them can be spinnaker (or cruising chute) guy/sheet blocks and lacing to the life-lines forward. This lacing prevents headsails from falling out through the life-lines when lowered.

Decks must be *non-slip*. In the author's opinion this is more important than toerails or life-lines. Quite simply the surface must either be wood, probably teak strip planking, or paint which includes sand or grit that provides plenty of friction for a wet rubber boot or shoe. Glass fibre is slippery even if moulded and so-called non-slip moulded patterns are *useless*. Paint over them with etching primer followed by proprietary deck paint (this has the sand ready mixed in it). What applies to decks also does to coachroof tops and hatches. If paint is not always used, then 3-M 'safetywalk' avail-

3.24 Good control for pulling mainsheet car to windward.

3.26 Hand holds essential.

able world wide can be stuck in any likely place. I use it on steps and critical points below as well. It is really hard and gritty – wonderful stuff!

Handholds should be adequate on deck. Quite simply there should not be anywhere that you cannot make a quick grab and find a firm hold (P 3.26). Standard teak hand rails made in the Far East seem to be on sale everywhere and a few more of these around is no bad thing. Such items on foredecks can double as toe

3.27 A steel rail near the mast can be a comfort in heavy going.

holds. The weight is acceptable and the windage is negligible. On large yachts an excellent device is the brace bar. This consists of a steel rail in way of mast or hatches to grab when working or moving in those areas. (P 3.27).

Life-lines are standard and once again they began in ocean racing. The racing rule height of 24 in (61 mm) is the norm with two lines running around the boat. Some cruising yachtsmen believe that 30 in (76 mm) is more seamanlike, but it places more leverage on base and fastenings. (Chapter 7). Pulpits and pushpits (stern pulpits) are designed for each boat, but the following points should be checked out on both pulpits and stanchions. They should be through-bolted and designed to take an outward strain (this affects the bolts on the base). Steel is preferable to aluminium, which eventually corrodes and fails. The tops must be of non-fouling shape so that headsails and lines pass across them without difficulty. 7 feet (2.1 m) is the maximum spacing between stanchions and pulpit uprights. The wires must be 'broken' with insulators or lanyards to prevent an induced magnetic field when using certain instruments for navigation. Pulpits and pushpits with openings are seen especially in Scandinavia and the Mediterranean for boarding fore and aft, but these should be

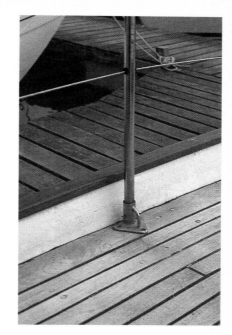

3.28 Conventional stanchion base with tang.

avoided if practicable. In any case they must be firmly shut with chain or wire and fool-proof catches. Life-lines and stanchions should not be expected to back up heavy gear and certainly not a man's safety harness (see Chapter 7), but their bases (P 3.28) can have beckets which should be able to withstand such loads.

It is the rig of any yacht which gives an immediate clue as to whether she is a slow cruiser, fast racer, vintage boat or has some special purpose such as crossing oceans shorthanded. For fast cruising there are three main requirements from the spars and sails: (1) *Power* on all points of sailing (2) *Comfortable* handling, though not necessarily always 'easy' handling and (3) Ease of *maintenance* and *reliability* at sea. If the rig does not meet these needs, it seems unlikely that it would be suitable for the fast cruising yacht.

Rig essentials

Power may be an obvious need, but the fact is that at highest speeds, the limit on performance is caused by the hull. (Chapter 1). More sail or more efficient sails cannot make the hull go beyond its maximum. On the other hand, in light and moderate winds, the hull has plenty of potential left in it, if only the rig can exert

drive. It is this ability to move in moderate winds that is so important. A yacht with 30ft (9.1 m) waterline and a theoretical maximum speed of 7.7 knots may in a true wind of 8 knots be close reaching at 3½ knots. Obviously she has plenty of potential left in the hull speed. To realize this needs more power for the same wind. So a more efficient rig could drive the yacht at, say, 4½ knots. On a one hundred mile passage she would make port 5 hours 3 minutes earlier. In tidal waters she might pick up a tide and make port ten or eleven hours earlier.

When sailing to windward, power of the rig is even more accentuated and is a vital ingredient for the cruising yacht. (Fig 4.1). If the wind is assumed to blow equally from every direction over a cruise or a season, then over one quarter of that time the yacht will be hard on the wind. When cruising, a fair wind is no 'problem'; sooner (usually) or later you reach

Fig. 4.1 For one quarter of the time a yacht is sailing to windward. This is shown by the assumptions that the wind blows equally from all quarters at some time, that the tacking angle is 90 degrees and that 12 degrees more free, still requires all windward qualities.

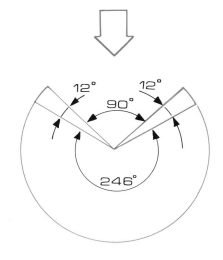

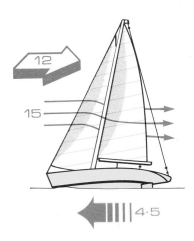

Fig 4.2 Sail area needs to be increased off the wind and how to do this easily is a problem for cruising. Here boat speed to windward of 4.5 knots gives 15 knots across the deck: down wind 6 knots gives only 5½ knots in the sails. True wind was 12 knots.

your destination, but upwind every yard gained to windward counts. The point being made is that exotic downwind rigs have their uses, but are not the priority for the cruising yacht. By contrast racing boats are on occasions designed to be off-the-wind fliers, for rating considerations and assumed wind directions on expected courses.

The cruising yacht does not need this excessive down wind sail area. In fresh winds it results in a 'hairy' ride with difficulty in steering and, quite frankly, a most insecure feeling. There is no need for a cruising yacht to be into a rhythmic roll which occurs when carrying a lot of sail, nearly straight down wind. Techniques for easing this include, for instance, taking the spinnaker sheet to a forward position. But if such a step becomes necessary, then the spinnaker would be better lowered. A boomed out genoa can go in its place.

Modern fin keel hulls are often blamed for the antics seen among ocean racers broaching or rolling heavily. There may be some truth in this, but the cause is more likely to be

a big spinnaker set from a tall mast (as the designer intended). Despite all these warnings, there must be provision to increase sail off the wind, because of the considerable drop in apparent wind on that point of sailing. (Fig 4.2). Ways of doing this are considered later.

To windward, however, performance is to be sought by the fast cruiser. It will be on a combination of the following: (1) Good helmsmanship or efficient self steering by vane or autopilot. (2) Weight kept to windward on board; for instance crew in the weather berths. (3) A rig that can be adjusted for strength of wind and state of sea; for instance, halyard tension and reefing arrangements (see below). (4) Well set up sails. (5) Well set up rigging. (6) Well made sails for windward work, not so old that shape has been lost. (7) Low windage (wind resistance) in the rig. (8) Stiffness, that is ability to stand up to the wind and carry sail. Stiffness (which is not the same as stability) comes from hull form, lack of weight aloft, low ballast and high ballast ratio – the

latter three giving a low centre of gravity.

Comfortable handling is at first obvious, for coping with the rig is the main activity apart from steering. It should have careful consideration. On racing boats handling has to be fast rather than 'comfortable', because there is manpower able to do the work. For fast cruising, the sail plan must be unencumbered, yet convenient to alter. When production boats are being advertised, the emphasis in the rig is very much on ease of handling. The advertisers appear to believe that this is what cruising people want most in their sail plan. One thinks immediately of furling genoas and a number of small sails rather than huge unmanageable ones. There are boats without headsails, staysails that tack themselves, boats without mainsails (the 'luna' rig), boats simply with short masts, maybe with junk rigs set on them. A point is that none of these go any faster: all are meant for comfortable handling. Comfortable handling seems to be on the opposite side of the equation to speed. Yet

50

apart from initial design there are all sorts of little ways in which sails and spars can be handled: we shall see some of these shortly.

Ease of *maintenance* is essential, for the rig is a place where it is often difficult to reach: when something goes wrong it may be unpleasant and dangerous to get (aloft) to it. The rig is a place for small split pins, potentially fatiguing metal and where unseen problems can grow. The logic is that if the components start simple there is less chance of trouble. Down below or on deck, it is often possible to get by with temporary arrangements, but in the rig it is much more difficult.

Only the steering gear and rudder are comparable to the rig in vulnerability combined with being vital for safety. There were once two advocates of rival dinghy classes extolling their respective merits. The first said that not one of the boats of the class had lost its mast in the last season. 'In that case', said his rival, 'your masts are too heavy'. This illustrates the quandry: exactly how 'fail-safe' should the mast be? In the 1981-82 Whitbread round the world race, there were a number of dismasting and rig failures, yet no one was hurt as a result. The fast cruiser looks as though it can afford to have a rig at the more solid end of the variation in such an ocean racing fleet.

It seems to be bad design more than actual slimming down on scantlings that is quoted as the reason for rig failures. Ah! But having rigging and mast walls, for instance that are a little heavier than the latest ocean racer allows for some bad design. And who can say that there is not some of that around in every boat!

At least most rigs can be ninety per cent inspected by eye. Watch for chafe, halyard sheave wear (sheaves should be easily replaceable aloft with the mast in the position), metal fatigue (some component or other bending back and forth), used again or unopened split pins (cotter pins). Toggles on rigging screws (turnbuckles) and regular inspections aloft by bosun's chair are basic and routine.

Common rigs

Most common yacht rigs are derived from racing either historically or because of recent fashion. (P 4.1). Latest extremes, in the early eighties, feature large mainsails, multiple spreader rigs and thin spars which have been controlled by several sets of backstays. Such rigs are a direct result of the current International Offshore Rule and what designers believe is the best performance under it. The ability of such rigs for cruising must be decided on merit. The fact is that they are bound to be pared down to minimum margins in weight and therefore strength: there is thus high dependence on crew work. This is not really for most cruising yachts; in many cases speed gains are marginal while rating gains are of no interest.

Of more practicality are rigs that acknowledge modern racing trends, but do not go the whole way with them. The current reversion to fractional rig is an example. It is quite acceptable for cruising to have two spreaders and a smaller headsail with spars that have a margin for error in their strength. One set of running backstays is enough; some racing boats may have more than this. (P 4.2).

4.1 Highly tuned racing rig.

thinner panels (P 4.4). As the intermediate shrouds must be in athwartships line of the mast it does mean there is no support at the upper spreader in a fore and aft line and a runner or preventer becomes advisable. On yachts under 35 ft (10.7 m) it is just possible to get enough support with a suitably designed mast section. The author has sailed with such a system in recent years and covered 10000 miles without accident. On one long passage in open water he had light weight runners rigged, but eventually never felt the need of them: the boat was 33.7 ft

4.4 Two spreader mast.

Designers may not realize that many rigs are derived from previous racing fashions or old rating rules. The common masthead sloop became established in the fifties under ocean racing rules of the CCA and RORC, but now would not be used for serious racing. The single spreader masthead sloop (or similar mast with a mizzen as well) has the attraction of simplicity (P 4.3), yet this is deceptive since the large foretriangle needs feeding with a variety of headsails and the largest ones will be a handful requiring large winches and space for stowage below. Also with only a single spreader it needs to be almost the same length as the beam of the boat at the mast, so sheeting in the genoa tight enough is difficult. On the credit side there should be no need for runners: setting up the rigging tension is not complex. For a sloop the height of the mast is what limits sail area in both main and foretriangle. (Fig 4.3).

Variations on this rig are those with two spreaders, allowing a thinner mast for better performance. The rigging supports the resulting

overall (10.3 m). In larger yachts he has used them when the sea condition demanded; that is when a heavy sea tended to make the mast 'pump'. This can be observed by looking up at the spar and watching its action. One way to alleviate 'pumping' is to force the mast into a bend (see below).

Multiple spreaders

Some racing boats with a masthead rig have three or even four sets of spreaders. It is not a cruising choice, but you may be fast cruising with such a spar. There are more linkages and the components are all thinner, especially the mast itself which is why there are so many sets of spreaders. With three sets of spreaders running backstays are essential (P 4.5) as well as the ordinary backstay to the top of the

Fig 4.3 To keep the rig inboard (i.e. no overhanging booms or bowsprits) only mast height enables sail area to be increased. Each of these sail plans is reasonable, but which is desirable?

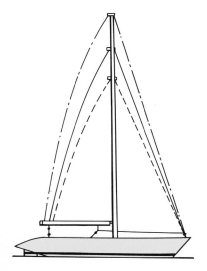

4.3 Simple single spreader rig.

mast. This is because the thin section held rigid by the multiple shrouds would otherwise compress into a bow and then break under the load of the masthead genoa. The 'runners' can well come to the same tackle at deck for handling, but this means an alert crew when tacking or gybing. Yet, it seems we are going down a path which is negative in terms of *handling* and *maintenance* and where *power* is too sophisticated for cruising. Two spreaders with or without runners seem to be the limit for cruising.

Mast bend

Like so much design and technique, mast bend owes its prevalance to rating considerations. Briefly, these concerned the area of the mainsail. A bent mast gave unmeasured area. Rules have been changed to make this less advantageous, but, as is so frequent in the history of yacht

design, the technique remains because it has been found useful for speed and not all that difficult to look after. Bending the mast flattens the mainsail, which is needed going to windward in a breeze. It can help to 'depower' the mainsail in a squall, so that the boat is less pressed. Conversely straightening out the mast makes the main fuller, to cope with getting the boat moving, when there is little wind but a choppy sea trying to slow her.

Masts that bend in this way are of the small section elliptical heavy wall type, rather than large section thin wall with 'delta' or 'bullet' shape sections. (Fig 4.4). The heavy wall mast is no lighter, but this is not often a factor under rating rules; what it gives is less windage and so an aerodynamically more efficient rig. Aluminium stiffening may be used

4.5 Triple spreaders for offshore racers.

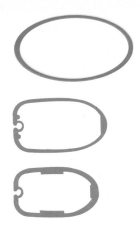

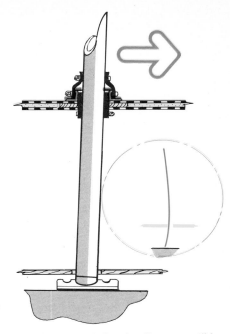

Fig 4.4 Elliptical mast sections are common, but modern sections that can be bent to assist rigidity are delta shaped, small overall section with thick walls. Reinforcement allows an even smaller section.

slightly forward from the keel to the mast partners at the deck (Fig 4.6). The backstay is set up to achieve this. The babystay is tautened, but as a 'steadier' as otherwise it adds unnecessary compression to the mast. The same principle applies to the runners: do not overtighten. For stronger winds tighten the backstay further, but to a limit previously decided, say, 6½ inches (160 mm) of bend for this size of boat. At this stage the mast will be quite rigid, its bend installed and so there is no tendency to pumping and therefore failure due to metal fatigue. Obviously this kind of mast is more likely to move around if it is left straight.

Double head rig
Many years ago single masted yachts with two headsails set at the same

Fig. 4.6 Below decks a bending mast will be sloping forward (forward indicated by arrow) so that it takes up curve above. Position is fixed at heel; deck wedges of very hard rubber held by clips are at deck level.

inside the section to beef up the fore and aft stiffness.

Mast makers often describe the strength of a mast section by its 'moment of inertia'. (Fig 4.5). This is the area of the material that is distributed from the neutral axis times the square of the distance it is positioned from that neutral axis. So it is a combination of thickness and 'diameter' and you can imagine a small thick walled spar having the same strength as another large diameter thin walled one. But windage and weight will be very different. There are in practice different moments of inertia on the fore and aft ('y') axis and the athwartships ('x') axis, since modern spars are never circular.

How much bend? In light winds and smooth water going to windward about 4 inches (100 mm) is right on a 35 ft (10.7 m) mast head rig yacht. The mast should slope very

Fig 4.5 Moment of inertia (the 'strength') of a mast section. It is the area of the section times the distance of its centroid from the axis; the resulting figure is in cm^4 or $inches^4$. So the thicker and 'wider' the section, the greater the 'strength'. It is a key figure in mast selection. This section could be 155 x 105mm. Wall thickness is 3.05mm. Weight 3.5 kg/m. Moments of inertia: Ixx 385cm^4 Iyy 179cm^4.

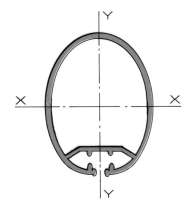

time were called cutters and were more efficient than sloops as it was possible to ensure the leading edges were taut. Modern materials now enable us to get a single large headsail setting well, but especially when the genoa is more than 500 sq ft (4657 m²) a double head rig means better ease of *handling* and it is very practical for fast cruising. For such a rig there is only one possible mast design: double spreaders and a running backstay to counteract the pull of the stay and halyard of the inner headsail (the staysail). (Fig 4.7).

Fractional rig

This again is a modern version of something quite old. Before 1950 the genoa and spinnaker seldom were attached more than seven-eighths of the way up the mast. Then came masthead rigs with the lower halyard block being rediscovered again in the seventies for racing boats and known as 'three-quarter' rig, 'five-sixths' rig and so on − hence the fractional rig. The modern spar is very flexible and highly tapered. This enables extreme bend to be obtained, as has long been the case on day keel boats such as the Star class. In such racing classes the technique has been well known for years, but now offshore the racers are using the same methods and so 'are sailed like dinghies...'. The relatively large mainsail is flattened and feathered by the bending mast in strong winds. The top of the mast flexes in squalls, thus easing the mainsail leech just when it is wanted, tightening it again as required when the wind moderates. This gives efficient power and has the added advantage that headsails are smaller than in masthead boats so more easily *handled* and winches are lighter.

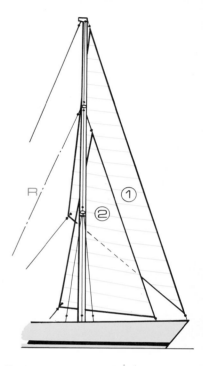

Fig 4.7 Double head rig with yankee (1) and staysail (2). Runner, R, is essential to support staysail stay.

The problem is that the mast is poorly supported because the backstay transmits its load only through the flimsy topmast; the running backstays have to be set up with precision that does not apply to the masthead rig. So critical is this handling of the runners when tacking, gybing and in certain conditions of wind and sea that the rig is unsuitable for cruising in its comtemporary form. Yet the small headsail with controllable efficient mainsail is undeniably an attractive concept for fast sailing. (P 4.6).

Swept back spreaders

There is a solution, though like all aspects of yacht design it has some drawbacks. The trick is to have swept back spreaders. (P 4.7). They

4.6 An easily handled fractional rig.

will be back at around 27 degrees. Thus the forestay is tensioned by the swept back shrouds Fig 4.8) and no runners are necessary. Yet the forestay on such a rig does not have the positive pull of a runner, only the very oblique tension of the main shrouds: the result is that the forestay will sag when going to windard which is all wrong for good windward performance. To try and get some form of tension in the forestay, the shrouds have to be heavily loaded (tightened) and this means that the rig is not suitable for yachts more than LOA 37 ft (11.3 m) at the most. Off the wind there is another problem, as the swept back rigging stops the main boom from being squared off as desired. When the mainsail is eased away, then there is chafe of the sail continuously.

A variation of this arrangement is the Bergstrom and Ridder rig (patented) which has been around for some years now and has been used on certain production boats, especially in the USA. The masthead rig has double swept back short spreaders with a diamond pattern of shrouds (Fig 4.9). This stops the mast bowing forward or bending sideways, so when he load comes on the forestay from the genoa, it directly loads the backstay. The mast can be lowered in one piece with all its rigging left at a tuned tension. The Bergstrom-Ridder is high on windage and quite a staunch section is needed to take all the compression that results; additionally there are a high number of linkages that need foolproof terminals and fitting.

Two masted rigs

All these types of mast could be joined by a second one on board to turn the sloop or cutter into a ketch, yawl or schooner. In practice it would on-

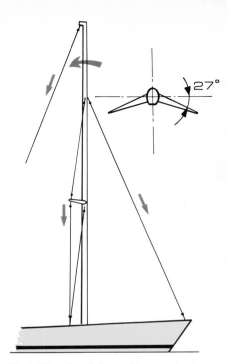

Fig 4.8 Fractional sloop with swept back spreaders at recommended angle. Though it obviates runners, it has some drawbacks.

4.7 Swept back spreaders cut into the mainsail.

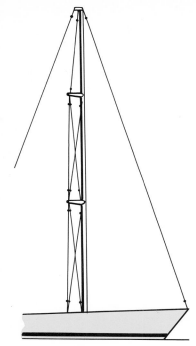

Fig 4.9 Bergstrom Ridder rig has multiple swept back spreaders and needs no inner forestay, nor runners.

short ends and rudder posts well aft mean that by definition a mizzen mast makes a ketch. Over 50 ft (15.2 m), the mizzen may split the sail area into worthwhile amounts, but below that size it is questionable if a ketch makes for fast cruising. To windward the mizzen barely overcomes the windage of its own spars and rigging. On a reach the mizzen fills, but as the wind draws aft it begins to blanket the mainsail! And do you really want to hoist a mizzen staysail in addition to a cruising chute (see below) and a big genoa or reaching headsail on the mainmast? And then find stowage for it later? How often have you seen a mizzen staysail (other than in photographs of ocean racing in the 50s — when the sail was there as unmeasured area under the rule). From this you see the author is not impressed with a second mast even if the mizzen does not come down and obstruct the cockpit nor the mizzen shrouds clutter the after

sidedeck. Nor is that weight aft conducive to speed, especially when it is being dragged along with no sail on it. (P 4.8).

Much of the same reasoning applies to schooners, but traditionally rigged gaff schooners with topsails make a fine sight at sea. Often such vessels (over 55 ft (16.8 m)) belong to training establishments or sailing schools — plenty of work for trainees! The practical application of the schooner and other two-masted rigs for fast cruising is in the use of special kinds of sail.

ly accompany a single or two spreader rig. Two masts split the sails up into easily *handled* units, but the rig has less *power* per square foot and there is more expense and less easy *maintenance* with more gear, fittings and linkages. Even the largest racing boats go in for single sticks. On the Round the World race of 1977-78 eight out of fifteen (more than half) of the boats were two stickers, but in the 1981-82 event only four out of the twenty-nine entries had other than a single mast. They were all big boats; some of them very big.

Few yawls are built today because

4.8 The mizzen: usually stowed.

5. Sail selection

Headsail problems

The headsail problem when cruising is at its greatest with the masthead rig, though slightly alleviated with the fractional rig. The difficulties are (a) excessive foredeck work to change sails which may be uncomfortable, exhausting and sometimes dangerous; (b) the temptation to carry the wrong sail and so slow down unnecessarily.

These disadvantages may be overcome by the following measures. (1) Careful *selection of inventory*; or (2) Using one of the widely available *furler-reefer headsails*; or (3) Having one of *the new rigs* which abolish conventional headsails, such as the Freedom, Gallant or Luna.

Inventory. Boats which habitually race will be found to carry selections of headsails which have been urged on their owners by sailmakers and yacht designers. It is difficult to reduce the number as it will tend to leave 'a gap'. For fast cruising conventional headsails can be reduced to the following.

No 1 or full size genoa with 1.5 overlap, but more for cruising in light airs.

No 2 or small genoa, flat and heavier cloth weight

Jib with exactly no overlap

Storm jib, emergency sail for winds in excess of 45-50 knots

Sails which are useless when cruising and indeed of doubtful value even when racing are the blooper/bigboy which is seen hoisted under it. There are running sails of great use: the spinnaker and/or cruising spinnaker (see below). As for the genoas and jibs, it is best of the area of these decreases in straight arithmetic proportions. On a 33 ft (10 m) masthead rigged yacht these might be: no 1 390 sq ft (39 sq m); no 2 280 sq ft (28 sq m); jib 170 sq ft (17 sq m) and storm jib 60 sq ft (6 sq m). So these come down about 110 sq ft (11 sq m) on each change. With fractional rig the storm jib is the same size for the same design of yacht, but the biggest genoa is obviously smaller. With this there comes the opportunity of cutting out even one more headsail, or at least making the changes less harsh with the same number of sails. Compare all this to the IOR limit on headsails for a yacht of 33 ft LOA, (10 m) which is seven including a 'heavy weather jib' and a 'storm jib'! For a yacht rating 30 ft

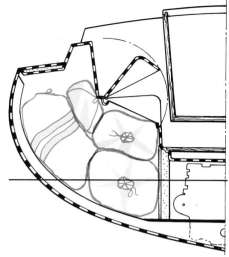

Fig 5.1 Sail bags convenient in large cockpit locker, but such an arrangement has potential danger.

(9.1 m) which is about 40 ft (12.2 m) LOA, the allowance is nine headsails before you even start on spinnakers. That lot needs some stowage.

Headsail changes and stowage

Once we have a cruising inventory of four headsails (or whatever is favoured for the size and type of boat), then changing them seems altogether an easier task. When cruising, a bareheaded change is best: it is not necessary to drive on to

5.1 Headsails hanked to twin stays permanently on deck.

windward quite so consistently (off the wind, there are fewer sail changing problems on the foredeck). If the sail is in a luff groove, it must be pulled straight down on deck and smothered, then bagged on deck if possible, thus entering the accommodation in an ordered state. The new sail bag is brought to the foredeck and lashed down before it is unzipped and the head of the sail inserted in the feeder to the groove.

If the sail is hanked to a wire forestay, then it is possible to leave an unused sail on deck, hanked below the sail in use and lashed down. Then if this sail is needed it is only necessary to unhank the sail in use after lowering it and up goes the sail that was previously on deck. For an able bodied crew there is much to be said for straightforward headsail changing in this way. Compared with furling systems, there is little that can go wrong and the resulting sail is the correct shape and size for the wind speed. (P 5.1)

A word on stowage. With the suggested restricted inventory, the problem is under control. Some yachts have large cockpit lockers for genoas not in use, but these may be so large that they drain into the bilge and such an arrangement is potentially dangerous (Fig 5.1). The weight aft is bad for performance. Another stowage is the fo'c'sle: it means that wet sails are away from the cabin, but is again means weight in an end of the boat and bow heaviness is even more undesirable than weight aft. So what about the main cabin? It is not such a stupid idea for you can walk over the sails in their bags and in heavy weather they provide safety in the form of cushioning. They can be grabbed quickly when wanted (as opposed to fumbling in the ex-

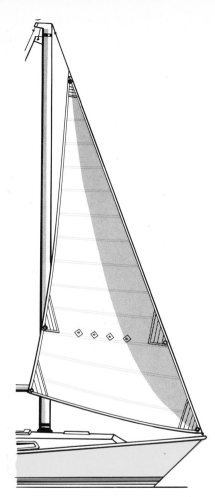

Fig 5.2 To cut down the number of conventional sails try a reefing headsail with panels to take the loads when reefed.

tremities of the yacht) and are in the optimum position low down amidships for performance. The storm jib (and the trysail) should have a distinct stowage, which is noted on the stowage list posted up in the cabin (Chapter 7). One additional tip for being able to reduce the inventory while carrying a selection of conventional headsails is the use of a jiffy reef in at least one headsail, probably in the no 2 genoa. (Fig 5.2). This gives two headsails for the price and convenience of one.

Furler reefer headsails
Furler reefer headsails are now in widespread use: so they must be considered by many as a solution to the problem of headsail changing and headsail stowage. The idea is not new; the practice of using roller jibs goes back one hundred years or more. They are never used on fully crewed racing boats so one must conclude that performance is not their strong point. Yet they are used on single-handed and short-handed racing boats, where far more time would be wasted in in trying to change headsails than is lost by reduced drive from the sail. Phil Weld (US) won the 1980 single-handed transatlantic race in *Moxie,* a 50 ft (18.3 m) trimaran using a Hood furling headsail and in the single-handed round the world race of 1982-83, Philippe Jeantot (France) had a double head rig in *Credit Agricole,* a 56 ft (17 m) monohull. The sails had a Pronengin furler on each headsail and his performance speaks for itself. Sailors like Weld and Jeantot and their advisers (designers, sailmakers, riggers) spent many hours to get maximum *performance* from their furling genoas and to ensure reliability, for there have been a number of recorded failures of similar systems in short-handed racing. Ease of *handling* follows. The average furler seen on cruising yachts looks a poor performer and the reason is well known (P 5.2). As the sail furls, it tends to become baggy and loose along its luff, the exact opposite to

5.2 A furled jib, but not very neat.

what is required. For quick stowage (the furling rather than the reefing aspect of the sail), there is every advantage except perhaps that concerned with the residual problem on boats of moving parts under tension and torque. There has been competition in recent years between manufacturers to win support of sailors, so for fast cruising there are at last several acceptable gears on the market. These are numerous, but mostly fall under one of the following ways of operation. (Fig 5.3).
Furling on own luff wire. This is a crude early system and impossible to tension once the headsail begins to roll up. Setting will be depressing, but the ordinary forestay remains free for conventional sails. Lowering the sail can involve it blowing overboard.

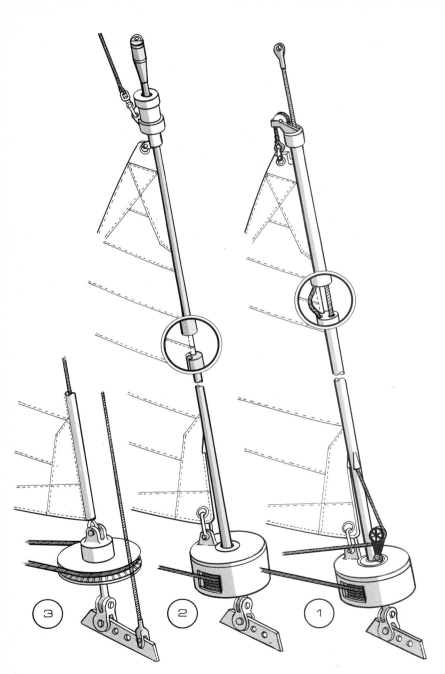

Fig 5.3 Variations of roller furler headsails. 1. Foil round conventional forestay and halyard down the foil and tightened on deck. 2. Solid foil forestay which turns, conventional halyard on a roller at top can be tightened hard on ordinary genoa halyard winch. 3. Roller sail independent of stay with endless line on drum; more suitable for inner staysails and small yachts.

Furling on a grooved foil, but with own halyard. The foil, or even a conventional forestay is on bearings both ends. The halyard passed up through a block on the forestay and down to a tackle at the base of the forestay. The whole system is then wound round. It is simple, but still difficult to get luff tension in strong winds.

Furling on a grooved foil, using yacht's halyard. This really is the one for best performance. The yacht's halyard can be used because it is linked to a roller which stays in position while the foil and the sail begin to roll. As with all the systems the sail is furled by hauling on a line from aft which rotates a substantial drum which turns the foil and the sail with it. To set the headsail, ease this line and haul on the sheet, or stop at any intermediate stage. A few designs have a continuous furling drum which resembles the self-tailing part of a winch, where a continuous line passes once around and is gripped by ridges inside the drum. Jamming and overrides are eliminated, but design is critical. Obviously each manufacturer has built in small features

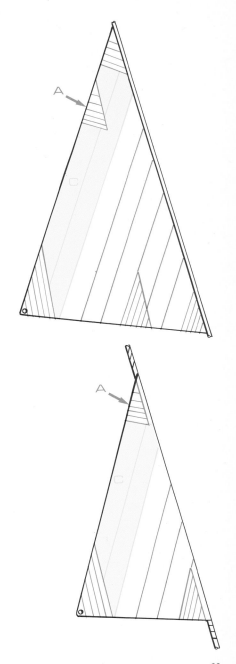

position must be as frictionless as possible via the accepted deck lead techniques.

Many of the manufacturers' grooved foils are also in use as conventional racing forestays and conversion kits are available. (P 5.2A). Thus the sail can be lowered and another headsail hoisted either on to the system, or, as is more likely quite separate from it. This is likely to be a large light weather sail which would not furl properly or the storm jib.

Furler reefer genoa cut
Ideally the furler reefer genoa is specially designed and cut. The principle is to place heavier sail cloth in the after part of the sail and as reinforcing panels at leech and foot. When the sail is partly furled reefed down to a small genoa size, then most of the exposed sail is of heavy flat cloth and reinforcement panels are close to the new head and tack. (Fig 5.4). A yankee in a double head rig furls better than a low cut genoa.

Alternative sail design
Having no headsails at all is an alternative approach. This usually involves unstayed masts with sails of novel shape and control. New systems are invented from time to time. They are enjoyable and certainly intended to be controllable, but are they fast? The main objec-

which are continuously developed, and for fast cruising the best quality equipment is advisable, as headsail problems are not what is wanted in a tight situation, nor loss of speed because of the headsail design. For instance the Hood 'Sea Furl' has a double swivel action, which causes the foil to begin rotating before the rollers at the head and track of the sail. This is intended to start flattening the centre of the sail first, taking out undesirable belly. It is not going to do this after the initial roll, so sail shape remains important. Some gears still have steel bearings, but these need heavy continuous lubrication and periodic replacement. Teflon or Delrin can be used instead, needing only a light oil spray occasionally. If the genoa is a lot shorter than the forestay a span should be inserted to get the top roller near the halyard exit, if not, the halyard may try to turn and so jam. Tension should be kept on the furling line at all times to avoid filling the drum interior, which could be another cause of jamming, perhaps just when sail is wanted in a hurry. The lead of the furling line to the cockpit, or after

Fig 5.4 It is difficult to get a furling head-sail flat as it is rolled in strengthening winds. Sailmakers try and cut sails to overcome this such as vertical cuts of heavier material (C) and reinforcement (A) at essential points.

tion is that they make for undercan-
vassed boats, which cannot spread
more sail off the wind when they
need it. In the 1982 race round the
British Isles, there were two
Freedom 35s. One of these was
equipped with a number of auxiliary
sails such as reachers, spinnakers
and between mast sails and came in
several days before her sister ship
after 1800 miles sailing. In other
words for fast sailing, the Freedom
had to carry and find stowage for
headsails.

The Freedom rig designed by Gary
Hoyt has free-standing masts – or
mast – constructed of glass and carbon fibre. (P 5.3). On these are set
'wrap-around' sails with wishbone
booms. All controls are led to the
cockpit and *handling* is made as easy
as possible. Later Freedom boats
such as the Freedom 39 have reverted
to a single ply sail. This is fully battened with a track up the mast in the
usual way. The booms (main and
fore in the schooner rig) are conventional aluminium. Lazy jacks doubl-

ing as topping lifts simplify reefing
and furling. By having the foremast
right in the bows, headsails are ex-
cluded. Boats with this rig have
made many excellent passages. The
designers do not pretend that the rig
is as close winded as a conventional
sloop, but comparisons are difficult
because many of these Freedom rigged boats have indifferent hull
shapes. A one-off big boat with the
rig, carrying three masts, wrap
round sails and wish bone booms,
the Freedom 70, did make the
passage Newport RI to south west
England in a mere thirteen and a half
days.

The Gallant rig is typical of at-
tempts seen from time to time to
achieve the same objects as the
Freedom design. (P 5.4). There are
aerofoil wishbone frames with wrap
round sails. The rig works well, but
there is no evidence that it increases
speed on any particular point of sailing. Because the frames hold the sail
cloth away from the mast, it is claim-
ed that it lowers more easily than the

Freedom when wet.

The Luna rig is designed by Dick
Carter (US) who has a fine record of
making conventional ocean racers
go very fast as a sailor and designer.
The rig consists of more than one
mast setting self tacking, high aspect
ratio jibs set on furler reefer gear.
(Chapter head). The problem of sail
shape when reefed is said to be overcome by varying the sheet lead of
each jib and, because there is no
overlapping headsail, steering, particularly self steering is said to be
simplified. The sail being ahead of
its mast rather than abaft is more efficient. The rig is probably most
suitable for sizable yachts; a 50 ft
yacht (15.2 m) was the first to be
built (the idea first appeared on the
128 ft (39 m) *Vendredi Treize*). In
smaller yachts one appears to be
doubling the amount of mast and increasing rigging to achieve the same
sail area as a simple masthead sloop.
It is not really mainsails in small
yachts that are difficult to *handle*.
Performance must suffer in the

Luna rig under 50 ft (15.2 m).

Mainsail speed

For all the special rigs and variation of headsails, there is much to be said for the conventional Bermudian (Marconi) mainsail, if only because it has been around so long and in such widespread use that it must be highly developed in terms of *power, handling* and *maintenance.* At the present time Terylene (= Dacron) is the best material for it in the fast cruiser. More recent materials are developing quite frequently, but often give improved performance (for instance holding their shape across a range of wind speeds) at the expense of very difficult handling and a propensity to fail suddenly. The latest advice must be taken when replacing a mainsail, as the situation keeps changing. There is no reason why the mainsail cannot make a strong contribution to performance, if the following aspects are looked after. *Mast thickness.* An over thick mast will interfere unduly with air flow

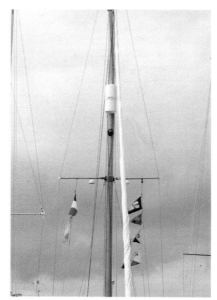

5.5 Mast clutter: permanent radar reflector, spreader lights, flags and heavy fittings.

over the mainsail; this makes a set of two spreaders preferable to single ones (see above). External halyards, flag halyards and various clutter (P 5.5) on the mast and rigging all decrease the value of the mainsail.

Original quality of design, cloth and cutting should be high. Reinforcing patches and fittings such as cringles should be hand sewn and material like hide used where applicable. A *luff groove* as used on racing yachts is faster and gets rid of the problem of slides which break off. It does mean that in masts over 50 ft (15.2 m) height there is a handling problem on lowering the sail. Slides on a track inside a shaped groove are then preferable. *Tensioning* for different conditions must be possible without difficulty. Winches should control the main halyard (it is better not sitting in a jammer), the leech Cunningham flattener and the clew outhaul. The kicking strap, (= boom vang), depending on the size of the sail, can be a solid or lever type controlled by a tackle. Hydraulics are not recommended as they are unduly powerful (causing damage), hard to *maintain* and costly. *All these controls are essential* and must be operated at all times for *maximum* power from the sail.

Reefing arrangements must be instantly operable. Three reef pennants should be rove at all times at sea, so the boom should have at least four exits at the tack (one for the clew outhaul) (Fig 5.5). The well tried jiffy reef system remains excellent and also delivers a well (flat) shaped sail and keeps the boom end high. To find the fixed position for the end of the pennant, have the leech of the sail bisect the angle of the pennant made by the block at the end of the boom − leech cringle − fixed end (Fig 5.6). The third reef should be a deep one and only leave fifty to sixty per cent of the length of the luff of the mainsail still exposed. A few small eyelets level with each reef enable reef points to be passed

65

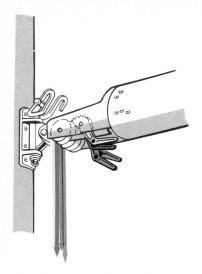

Fig 5.5 Tack exits. This fourfold arrangement can handle pennants for a clew outhaul and/or leech flattener and three reefs.

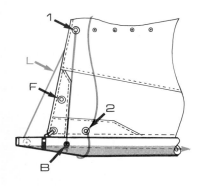

Fig 5.6 Reef leech cringles. To find position on boom make leech bisect angle of pennant (L) when leading from boom end block. F is flattener and 1 is first reef. Sometimes sailmakers insert cringles in foot so boom fittings are not necessary, nor need be altered, if a different mailsail is fitted. Second reef position (2) only shown for clarity.

5.6 Mainsail furling in the mast.

through to remove excessive sail cloth after reefing, but they are not essential to pulling down the reef. If these reef points are made of thin stuff, then if the sail is rehoisted without unreeving all of them, they will break and there is no danger of tearing the sail.

Furling mainsails

There are variations on the conventional mainsail, borrowing furling techniques developed in headsails. There are mainsails which can be furled by zip fasteners. A scoop at the masthead is pulled by a special halyard. There is a two ply luff with zippers sewn in the sail each side. The mainsail with its clew released gathers into the scoop and when this reaches the bottom the sail is completely furled into its protective cover. Of more practical application for fast cruising is the Stoway mast patented by Hood Sailmakers. The mainsail is reefed or furled by rolling it into the mast, in which there is an ample compartment kept clear of halyards, wiring and so on. (Fig 5.7). An endless line on a winch in the cockpit or elsewhere turns the roller; the specially arranged clew outhaul is eased and the sail area disappears into the mast. (P 5.6). It can be fitted to boats of 30 ft (9.1 m) or over. In both these systems, sail battens and

headboards cannot be fitted, which means less area for the given height of mast and obviously the mast itself or its fittings are not conducive to mainsail performance. Hood has taken this a stage further with a Stoway boom. At first sight it appears to be a return to the bad old days of roller reefing, but the special boom *into* which (not round which) the mainsail is rolled has a number of advantages. Headboard, sail battens and the ordinary mast with its groove are retained together with

Fig 5.7 Furling mainsails have proved dependable. The sail is rolled in a section quite separate for the duct for halyards and wiring.

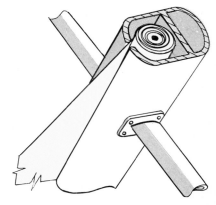

boom fittings such as kicking strap (= vang) and mid-positioned mainsheet.

Increasing area off the wind

As already implied, most of the 'convenience' rigs do not help as the wind draws aft, most of them lacking area, even on the wind in light to moderate conditions. The spinnaker is the conventional sail as soon as the wind draws abaft the beam (P 5.7). Rating rules mean that a spinnaker usually increases the working sail area by two-thirds or more. It therefore becomes demanding when the wind increases or draws ahead. It is also a fact that it requires a considerable amount of gear exclusively for its own use; this may include two halyards, two guys, two sheets, a foreguy, spinnaker pole, heel lift, topping lift, moveable inner forestay, pole stowage and jockey pole (reaching strut). No wonder for cruising, alternative systems are sought, but it must be said that none of these gives as much speed as the spinnaker. In moderate winds and smooth sea the spinnaker can knock hours off the passage.

The spinnaker sock goes under a number of names (chute-stuffer, snuffer, spinnaker sally, squeezer etc). This soft tube contains the spinnaker and is peeled away to hoist it,

5.8 Lowering a sock over the spinnaker.

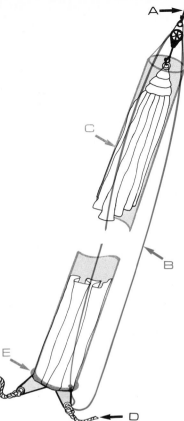

5.9 Cruising chute.

staying at the top of the sail when the latter is set. To remove the spinnaker sheets and guys are eased and the sock douses the spinnaker. Follow the instructions supplied with the various designs. (P 5.8). The sock does have rather a lot of strings and still has to be hoisted and lowered before and after the unpeeling or peeling, so it is also rather tedious. All the lines for the hoisted spinnaker are also required. (Fig 5.8).

An alternative is the cruising chute (also known as the genniker, spanker, coaster etc). Its advantage over the spinnaker is that the tack is secured to the stem head, giving immediately more stability and control. It is not as effective as the spinnaker and would be handed in a strong breeze. (P 5.9). Being asymetrical it is highly effective when reaching, but whereas the wind draws aft a conventional spinnaker can be trimmed aft, the cruising chute will collapse in the same way as a normal genoa (Fig 5.9). It is then

Fig 5.8 Spinnaker sock (there are various propietary names). A is yacht's spinnaker halyard; endless line, B pulls sock, C, up to reveal spinnaker, or down to smother it; the sock of Terylene (Dacron) has rigid mouth, E. Otherwise spinnaker has normal sheet, D, and other fittings.

Fig 5.9 A typical cruising chute has 40 per cent more area than the largest genoa (G), but 30 per cent less area than a full size spinnaker (S).

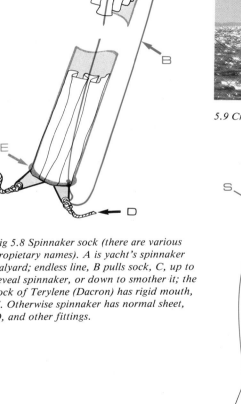

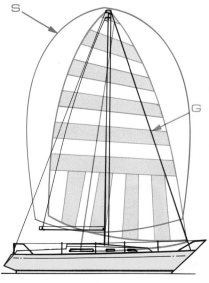

68

Fig 5.10 For cruising chute and genoa a telescopic pole is advisable, being longer than standard spinnaker pole. Some have internal tackles to adjust when in use.

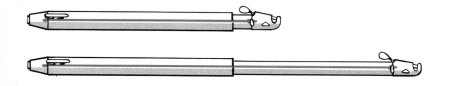

necessary to rig a pole, which is run to its clew. It is then like a boomed out genoa, but with more area, much of which is baggy. The pole needs to be longer than a spinnaker pole, indeed half as long again which is quite something. A telescopic pole may be useful to overcome stowage problems. (Fig 5.10). For effective poling out there must be a spinnaker halyard, separate guy and sheet (see below), a single mast fitting (mast heel lift is not needed), tack line on the sail tack (preferably through a block and then controlled from aft: down when reaching, up when running). A pole lift is required, but a foreguy is not essential as the tack line stops excessive lift (unlike a spinnaker which goes aloft out of control if the foreguy lets go). The cut of cruising chutes varies between sailmakers; each will say that his own computerized cut is the best yet. A customary size is the luff equal to the length of the forestay, width about 1.7 times base of foretriangle. Area is about thirty per cent less than a spinnaker. A spinnaker sock can be used with a cruising chute.

Booming out the genoa
In a fresh or strong wind aft the fast cruiser (sometimes the racing boat) can best boom out the genoa. Again an adjustable pole is preferable to an ordinary spinnaker pole. It is important not to put the genoa sheet through the end of the pole; a separate guy should be used. This stricture also applies to the boomed out cruising chute. This is in order to ensure safety when bringing in the pole, the load being taken on the

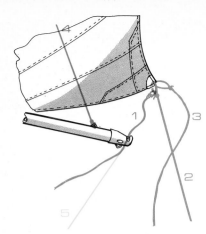

Fig 5.11 Safe way to boom out genoa (or cruising chute) is to use conventional spinnaker gear. Rig spinnaker guy (1) through pole end, so when dropping, sheet (2) is taken up and (1) released without strain. 3 is lazy genoa sheet (not on cruising chute). Control pole with topping lift (4) and fore guy (5).

sail's own sheet and then the guy slacked to ease the pole to the deck using the topping lift. (Fig 5.11).

In order to increase ordinary area without the use of a spinnaker, remember a second headsail can be hoisted using complete spinnaker gear, assuming this equipment is rove already. (P 5.10).

There are of course a number of other traditional down wind systems, including squaresails and twin running sails on twin poles. It must be remembered that if these demand spars and heavy gear at all times on deck and aloft, they can only slow down the yacht when going to windward and so are not readily conducive to what is envisaged here as fast cruising.

6. When the going gets tough

In this section we speak of 'tough' weather rather than 'bad' weather. There is discussion of what happens in strong wind and in fog. Neither of these are all 'bad', since as the going gets rough, sailing can be more fun and even fog is exciting to navigate successfully. And who has not sat in a calm and said 'I would rather have a gale than this.'?

Such exhilaration is not likely to last long and heavy weather brings in due course weariness and apprehension. I can think of two vivid examples. One was the Fastnet storm of 1979. As the wind piped up on that fateful night, we pulled down reefs and the able crew said 'This is what we came for.' A gale was part of the scene. Later it was different as the gale turned to storm and news of casualties came over the radio. The second example was on a more lighthearted cruise, which began in very fine, hot weather. As we beat to windward, the breeze and sea piped up and shorts and shirts remained the order of the day. As spray tipped over, some in the cockpit laughed and shouted in the cold shower; yet in the space of forty-five minutes at least one of the crew was suffering mild hypothermia and had to be helped below and wrapped in a sleeping bag. The lesson seems to be to enjoy the initial challenge of the gale, but do not take it lightly. Tough can quickly get rough.

When does it get tough?

What constitutes tough going varies immensely. The human factor is very large, but the abilities of different sorts of crew are facts which are too late to change once the gale blows. The length of the cruise is something that can be taken into account. That is to say the crew will be able to stand more punishment if it has been fast cruising for several weeks, than in the first few days at sea, or on short passages. For instance a round-the-world racer sails on in almost any conditions, while a yacht out with a raw crew may hit force 6 on leaving harbour and its skipper may feel the need to put straight back to port.

Wind strength is not the whole story and the factors which make conditions tough or not include (a) the size of the yacht, (b) whether sailing up wind or down wind, (c) the temperature of air and water, (d) how much the land shelters, for instance if the boat is near a weather shore or not, similarly what is the fetch (the distance travelled by the wind from a weather shore or from where the wind starts to blow), (e) the state of the sea, which will often be partly due to (d), but may also be affected by currents and tidal streams, uneven soundings, sudden wind changes and even inexplicable variations. One hears 'There was not all that amount of wind, but the seas were really nasty'. Or by contrast 'It was blowing 45 knots, but there was

71

Fig 6.1   WHAT FACTORS MAKE
CONDITIONS TOUGH

Large yacht	Small yacht
Sailing down wind	Sailing up wind
Small fetch	Long fetch (distance of land to windward)
Regular sea	Difficult sea (uneven bottom, currents etc)

Score 5 for each factor in left column and 10 for each in right and the higher the total the worse the conditions e.g. small yacht (10), down wind (5), small fetch (5), difficult sea (10) is 30. When the wind heads score is 35, but when sea becomes regular it is back to 30!

surprisingly little sea'. Fig 6.1 shows this as a table.

To consider heavy weather, it is necessary to draw an arbitrary line between *gale conditions of around force 6 to 8* on the one hand and the *storm conditions of force 9 and above*. (Fig 6.2 for wind strengths). In the gale, if the fast cruiser is already at sea, she can keep going. In the more severe storm conditions there is a strong preference to seek shelter, but if this is not practicable, then it is necessary to survive at sea. In the conditions of force 8 and below, the skipper can also opt to seek shelter, but this is not specially desirable and does not require any unusual techniques of seamanship. Note that Chapter 7 of this book looks at emergency and safety equipment and fitting out and the use of such gear and so should be read in conjunction with these thoughts on tough conditions.

Gale conditions

Of course, no one can tell that force 6, 7 or 8 will not get even stronger, but the stronger forces in summer are less common. Preparations are the same: it is only that certain further urgent actions may be needed in severe (the word will be used here to indicate force 9 and higher) conditions.

There may be warnings of the approaching gale by a rapidly falling *barometer*, forecasts by *radio* or by *sea and swell* building up more than the wind warrants. Here is a rule for the rate of fall of *barometer* which is very useful (and also reassuring, if it does not fall at such a rate.)

Fall per hour	Expected wind force
2 mb	6
3 mb	8
6 mb	10 - 12

In order to spot such falls, the barometer must be read every hour at least and entered in the log book with other navigational data (see Chapter 8). Better still is a barograph trace giving by its gradient an immediate warning (Fig 6.3). The barograph is even more useful for long term weather forecasting, since one is unlikely to record barometer readings over a period in harbour, while the barograph has it all there to see.

Radio forecasts are usually widely publicized in each country where they operate. Dependability has improved in recent years owing to the uses of satellites, computers and other modern aids. The author believes that many forecasts are still inaccurate about wind strengths: the reason for this is that few occupations demand to know the wind (unless it is extreme) and yachtsmen are in a minority in wondering which it will be: 17 or 25 knots! Time and again, everywhere in the world, it turns out wrong. Meteorologists will score good results and then say that the forecasts were, say, 85 per cent correct. Yet this does not help you on the specific occasion that you put to sea and twelve hours later run into an unannounced gale. It is fair to say that the really severe gale is very often not forecast (similarly forecasts gales may not materialize). The moral, as known by experienced cruising men is to listen to the forecast and then be ready for anything. Once you are fully confident of coping with the unannounced, then it is not necessary for adverse forecasts to curtail your plans. Gales are frequently localized and conditions can be quite different twenty miles apart: the radio forecast often cannot handle this sort of thing.

In these days of radio warnings and satellite observation, *swell* is on-

Fig 6.2   DEFINITIONS OF STRONG WINDS, GALES AND STORMS REFERRED HERE AS 'GALE CONDITIONS' FOR 6 TO 8 AND 'STORM' FOR FORCE 9 AND ABOVE

BEAUFORT FORCE NUMBER	KNOTS (MEAN SPEED)	METRES PER SECOND (MEAN SPEED)	DESCRIPTION
6	24	12	strong breeze
7	31	16	moderate gale
8	37	19	gale
9	44	23	strong gale
10	54	28	storm
11	60	31	violent storm
12	64	33	hurricane

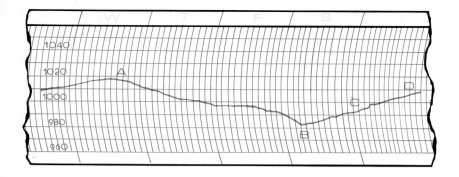

ly a second class warning of an approaching gale. It is more reliable away from the shore and in practice will be of greater use when away from coastal radio forecasting. Swell is the word given to waves over which the wind has been blowing when they leave the area in which they were generated. As we know the wind can be very light, but the swell may be big. The height of the swell depends on how long the wind has been blowing, on the fetch (distance from the generating wind), on currents and on present wind strength. Swell decreases as it distances itself from the generating area.

The probable mean wave height in the open sea in a gale when the wind has been blowing steadily (which it seldom actually does) is as follows. Force 6 = 10 ft (3 m); force 8 = 18 ft (5.5 m); force 10 = 30 ft (9 m). These figures may increase to a probable maximum of fifty per cent more, so force 8 could without exception be 27 ft (7.5 m) and force 10 be 45 ft (12.5 m) and that is big! There may be plenty of exceptions and these figures are a guide.

Such waves depart from the generating area and the swell (which they now are) gives to the yacht crew an indication of the distance from the edge of the storm, how long the swell took to get from there and the wind speed in the generating area. All these help to let you know what sort of weather is on the way and the strength of the wind when it arrives (if it does). The graph in Fig 6.4 gives answers on the distance, time taken and generating area wind speed, by observing the height and period of the swell. The period is a complete cycle (e.g. top of one wave to the next in seconds) and the height of a wave be it sea or swell, is from the trough

Fig 6.4 How swell can be related to weather at a distance. Red lines indicate distance which swell has come (figures in nautical miles), yellow show travel time in hours, blue lines are wind speed in generating are in knots. H is height of swell ft/metres; P (bottom line figures) is period of swell (see Fig 6.5) in seconds.

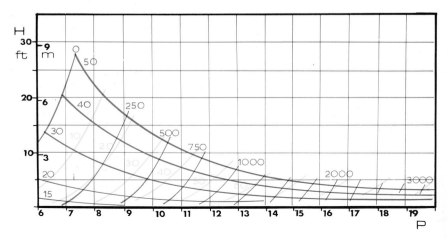

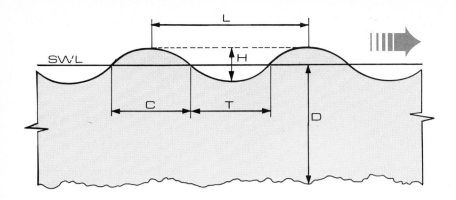

Fig 6.5 How to describe ocean seas and swells. L, wavelength of sea or swell; H, wave height; C, wave crest; T, wave trough; SWL, still water level, D, depth to sea bed.

to the crest (Fig 6.5).

So much for warnings, which should also include yachtsman's meteorology which comes from practice as well as signs in the sky, a knowledge of weather types, observation of the pattern over the last week or two and information on the character of the weather in the particular area and time of year. As for theory, there are many manuals on weather; it has the advantage of being a subject that can be studied at other times than when at sea.

With winds of gale force expected here is a list of preparations that should be made on board.

Crew. Put on heavy weather clothing, including thermal underwear and also harnesses.

Cook. The cook makes a hot meal before conditions deteriorate. Hot food can be put into containers. Emergency food to be made readily available, such as biscuits, chocolate and tea. It will not then be necessary to 'rummage' in difficult conditions.

Navigator. The dead reckoning position should be brought up to date and fixes taken before the weather deteriorates. These may be by electronic, celestial or terrestrial means. Check out electronic and electric equipment and charge batteries if required. Note times of upcoming radio weather forecasts. Record barometer at frequent intervals (or observe barograph).

Around the deck. Hoist radar reflector (visibility will be bad and hoisting it would be one more difficult task in strong winds). Check mainsail reef pennants rove off, especially the third one and lead to winch ready. Halyards and other gear unlikely to be used (e.g. spinnaker halyard) to be made up and secured so they cannot fly out or wash away. Check (if used) sea anchor and warp for streaming. Check washboards and/or companionway entrance from on deck (for devices see Chapter 7). Check security on any cockpit lockers. Pump and sponge bilge completely dry.

Down below. Close sink and lavatory sea cocks (but not engine cooling inlet cock). Have smaller headsails and storm canvas more readily available for bringing quickly on deck (but locations may already have been marked, see Chapter 7). Fix strong backs to hatches. Shut off ventilators as necessary. Check stowage of gear that could be dislodged on excessive heeling or knock-down. Heavy gear which could cause injury to be restowed, if necessary. Check anchorage of batteries, anchors and other heavy gear. Check washboards and companionway entrance from below and insert boards etc early to avoid heavy water getting below.

During the gale

For the capable fast cruiser, *going to windward* in winds up to force 8 in the open sea will be harder on the crew than the boat. Once canvas has been reduced, perhaps with three reefs and the 'no 4' jib, the one just a size bigger than the storm jib, short watches are the best with at least two persons on deck, both of them being on short harness spans with anchorages inside the cockpit. If hot food can be served up at times so much the better. I can recall times when a cook has produced hot meals in such conditions, but it is five times the hard work in moderate breezes because of the angle of heel, the heat and steam in the galley because of being battened down, the difficulty of keeping pans on the stove due to motion and subsequently passing hot food or liquid safely up. Such aids as instant soups and disposable (biodegradable) cups and plates are useful to cope. Then there have been times when hot food for a few hours or longer is not practicable, yet remember it is not essential to have food hot, so cold ready-use foods can be consumed.

Seasickness, if it affects a number of the crew, can be a serious problem. I believe that most persons become immune after periods at sea, or even if they sail every week-end during the season. Some persons, however are always affected and I regret to say that you take them fast cruising at your risk! As skipper or watch master, look for anyone who feels suddenly sleepy, yawns a lot or looks pale (even slightly green) in the face. Other precautions which I try and take are to encourage members of the crew to eat simple meals before the voyage, avoiding alcohol and fatty foods. Crew should take drugs which suit them, not merely when bad weather approaches. Most drugs need to be taken a couple of hours 'before journey' and then regularly afterwards. It is not proposed to specify drugs here, because names vary in different countries and different people have preferences. In some places effective drugs can be bought over the counter and elsewhere a doctor's prescription is essential. Brands containing *dramamine* and *hyoscine* have been common for many years, but in the seventies pills of *cinnarizine* as used for ear troubles became available and these proved effective for many who had found the other pills no use. Since seasickness is believed to be caused by the upset of the balance facilities in the human ear, then it is not surprising that the latter drug is significant. As drugs may cause drowsiness, they are best taken at the end of a watch. Plaster or straps behind the ear and on the wrists have been tried and reported on, as has hypnotism. From time to time other methods of prevention are spoken of, but personal trial or direct recommendation is the only sure test.

If the boat is *off the wind,* it is tempting to carry too much sail as the wind increases. However modern boats with the rudders right aft will steer well; heavy tiller or wheel pull indicates too much sail. Actually in force 8 a modern yacht off the wind is likely to be at maximum speed and sail can be cut right down early. When running nearly dead down wind, the question arises whether to rig a boom vang to stop an accidental gybe (P 3.16). The problem is that if the yacht does gybe with a vang, she is liable to be pinned down with the main boom held amidships (Fig 6.6). Consider allowing the main boom to slam across, if it has to, but *heads down* at all times and substantial stops and limited reach on the main sheet traveller are needed (P 3.24).

When changing down to *minimum sail,* several important points arise, which can be resolved by careful planning. On masthead rigs, if the storm jib is set without the mainsail (even for a time, for instance when reefing or experiencing some trouble with the mainsail) beware that mast security without the mainsail acting as a partial stay. Runners and inner forestay should be set up. On fractional rigs the runners should be set up. (Fig 6.7). The sheet lead positions must have been fixed in advance and this is certainly one time when the leads must not slip (Chapter 3): there will be a tendency to slip because of the upward pull of a jib, rather than a genoa. In the mainsail certain problems arise with a third reef. As there are only two luff hooks, at the tack the first reef may

Fig 6.6 A gybe with a vang (V) can mean being pinned down and unable to gybe back.

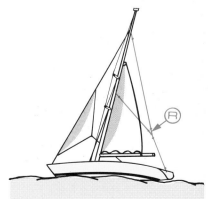

Fig 6.7 With the mainsail heavily reefed — or even removed completely, support normally given by the mainsail 'against' headsails disappears. Runners (R) must be kept fully set up.

6.1 One reef down, but a lot more cloth to come for second and third.

Fig 6.8 Chart table essentials for rough weather. A. Navigator's belt (when to windward). B. Athwartships book case. C. Spray curtain (when to leeward). D. Very deep fiddle to hold charts and books in use. E. Instrument rack.

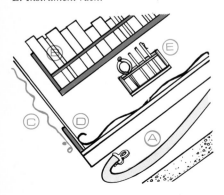

have to be unhooked, but the resulting slack should be held by reef points. If the boom has multiple reef pennants/clew outhauls (Fig 5.6) the third reef can be pulled straight down, but otherwise a messenger will have to be connected to the end of the disconnected first reef pennant and used to haul this through the clew cringle at the third reef level. Finally when the reef has been pulled down, reef points must still be available (remember quite a number have been used already) for the third reef which is the deepest and has much loose cloth to gather up. (P 6.1).

Navigation in heavy weather

If the chart table arrangements are well organized as explained in Chapter 8, then they will function in force 8 or higher wind speeds. Certain difficulties are accentuated in bad weather and these are as follows. It is difficult physically to stay at the chart table, which should work at an angle of heel and have a strong belt for the navigator (Fig 6.8). Water will drip off the navigator if he has just come below: charts can soon be reduced to the state of wet pulped newspaper! So dry off first and have plenty of tissue for mopping up (yes, there are charts printed on waterproof, tearproof paper (PVC) and this product is also useful for notices pinned to the bulkhead etc). Well sited chart area and spray guards come into their own in this weather. Visibility may be bad owing to boat movement, actual poor visibility at a distance which is the case on frontal systems and owing to driving rain and spray. Terrestrial and celestial position lines will often be impossible. Careful dead reckoning should therefore be kept. This in turn means working at the chart table without

being affected by seasickness. Some crew are prone to this when working on a chart, while they may not otherwise be affected. A fast cruiser will have a navigator who can crouch over a chart in all weather! Of course, this is where electronic position finding systems are very valuable indeed and are the surest means of checking the position in such weather. They should not however be depended on as an excuse to run to harbour. A fairly recent case in New Zealand involved a yacht running for shelter in a severe gale using Satnav and striking a rock on her course inward. Counting on such accuracy caused most of the crew to be lost. There will be considerable drift and leeway, whatever the tactics in the gale and the navigator must make ample allowance. (P 6.2).

On a weather shore or with comfortable searoom, the only basic problem is a wind shift, but on a lee shore a calculation should be made

Fig 6.9 Seeking sea room. Yacht 15 miles off lee shore takes best tack for three hours to make this 30 miles.

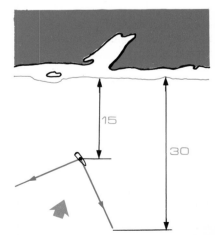

as to how long the yacht can drift to leeward, if the gale should get any stronger. If, say, 15 miles offshore with no safe harbour available, it is worth getting on the tack to take you most quickly away from the shore (Fig 6.9). Three hours of this with a gale increasing to force 8 would mean (depending on the size of yacht) a total of 30 miles offshore. This is beginning to get more secure in the event of even severer conditions pushing you towards the coast. Hove-to making 2½ knots leeway, gives you 12 hours away from the shore (or rather the known outlying dangers). More on this topic in a moment.

Storm conditions

Now we shall look at the serious problems that can arise when the wind is force 9 or even higher in exposed waters. 44 knots or more; 23 metres per second or more. For long distance voyaging, sooner or later such wind strengths will be met, but for a fast cruiser in the summer season in customary yachting areas of the world it is rare. The fact is therefore that at any time there are only a few people with experience of being caught out in storm force winds and many other yachtsmen with no such experience. They have to listen to those who have had experience of such weather, hope they will not meet it, but be prepared to cope with it if they do.

The size of the yacht has much to do with it and round the world racers, even when sailed single-handed are as large as possible, usually over 60 ft (18 m). In 1970, a steel

6.2 Entering harbour must be visual day or night, rather than reliance on electronic aids.

Fig 6.10 Some recorded knock-downs of different types of yachts, but there are some forty well recorded cases of many different types. (Multihulls of which many have 'flipped' not recorded here).

Name of yacht and type	Area	LOA ft	Beam ft
Adventure (IOR 70s)	South Atlantic	55	14.4
Dubloon (old CCA rule) centre board	North Atlantic	39	10.9
Galway Blazer (light single-hander low rig)	Off Cape of Good Hope	43	10.5
Joshua (heavy single-hander)	Southern Ocean	39.5	12.0
Tzu Hang (heavy double ender)	Southern Ocean	46.0	11.5
Trade Wind (modern heavy cruiser	Bay of Biscay	33	10.6
Trophy (moderate IOR)	Fastnet '79	37	11.0

yacht of this size, specially built, set out from England to sail the 'wrong way' round the world; that is *eastabout* against the wind through the southern ocean. The boat was sailed single-handed by Chay Blyth without stopping and returned to her home port after 292 days. The point is that this modern strong boat with a separate keel and rudder, beat into winds of force 10 on a number of occasions. It therefore can be done and since then boats have improved in construction and a few have even bothered to repeat the voyage. (But most voyagers and all races go the 'right' way).

For smaller boats and less hardy crews, beating in such conditions is not advisable (unless the seas have for some reason remained small, for instance at the height given for force 7-8 above) and there are two main tactics to adopt. These are: (a) *(hove-to or fore-reaching* under trysail and storm jib, or (b) *running before* the storm. Details of both these resorts will be discussed.

What is now considered very unwise is to lie a-hull. Yachts will look after themselves for hour after hour with the helm lashed and drifting sideways. The crew can go below in warmth and comfort, but in the open sea in force 9 or above, a breaking wave may overwhelm the yacht turning her beyond horizontal, with a strong possibility of structural and gear damage and crew injury. When using methods (a) and (b), this can still happen, but lying a-hull is asking for it. There is an eerie sameness to the reports of these knockdowns and capsizes. The crew invariably report that all is well, perhaps in their bunks below, perhaps running before the storm with no problems. Then quite suddenly their whole

world is upside down, crew flung from their bunks, equipment flying and water squirting through hatches. Damage or flooding ensues. The Fastnet race of 1979 has been much quoted for examples of storm conditions. The facts are that of the 303 starters, 85 finished the race and the remainder retired, many without any damage or injury. However 15 persons were drowned and 19 boats were abandoned, all of which were recovered except 5. The fleet represented the latest ideas in offshore racers at that time. The author was in one of the yachts and believes that if the same number of average 'slow' coastal cruisers had been in the same position (which they would never be in such numbers) the rate of damage, loss and casualties would have been far higher. There were in fact losses on cruising yachts in the area, but these were unpublicized. The racers were subjected to an enquiry, 33 per cent of the skippers answering a questionnaire reported a knockdown to beyond horizontal. From the way the enquiry was conducted it is difficult to measure, but probably more than 30 boats were completely rolled over in the seas and six of these were between 44 ft (13.5 m) and 55 ft (17 m). There was no immediate relation to being capsized and to boat type. It is something that can happen to any sailing yacht whatever her shape and ballast.

Away from the Fastnet and in different parts of the world, there are numerous recorded knockdowns. In the table (Fig 6.10) widely different types are shown to have suffered. *Joshua*, the very heavy, steel, ketch sailing one and a half times round the world by Bernard Moitessier had, as has been mentioned, seven knock downs beyond horizontal, four of which went to 130 degrees; one knock down for every 5000 miles! His voyage was mostly in the southern ocean. By contrast *Rock 'n Goose* , an Irish racing sloop of 28.3 ft (8.6 m), was turned through 360 degrees 50 miles off La Rochelle in the Bay of Biscay, losing her mast in the process. She returned to port unaided.

The most likely dangers in a knock down, whether nearly horizontal, horizontal, or beyond are (a) dismasting, (b) other damage above deck, (c) shipping water of lesser or greater amount (d) equipment below deck causing damage (e.g. smashing windows) or injuring the crew (e) crew injury. A number of the security measures in the next chapter are intended to reduce these risks, but for (a) there is little to be done except ensure the rig is sound. Masthead instruments will likely be lost, so spares should be carried. To prevent (b) basic structural integrity is the best safeguard. There have been cases of rudder skegs (Fig 6.11) twisting away from the hull and causing leaks almost impossible to control (in 1983 the yacht *Montego Bay* off New Zealand and *Adfin's Rival* in western approaches to British Isles: fatalities in both cases). Chapter 2 has discussed whether an independent hung rudder is safer in this respect? Watertight integrity (c) is partly constructional design and partly ensuring wash boards and other entrances are *closed early* . The 55 ft (16.7 m) *Adventure* shipped 200 gallons (891 litres) of water when she was knocked down horizontal in the south Atlantic with a top wash board only unshipped. For (d) secure all possible items. To avoid crew injury, there should be no sharp corners on

mouldings, lee cloths on bunks must not burst open and remember flying food tins have caused injury. Sails wedged in the accommodation can provide padding and why have a steel box for tools anyway? They are safer in canvas rolls

Positive steps in a storm

It is not possible to be dogmatic about the best course of action in any particular storm and for any special boat or crew. These views are offered as being quite widely accepted. Some skippers may care to use them as a starting point.

Is does seem that keeping the boat moving is highly preferable to 'stopping'. Lying a-hull we have already cautioned against. The traditional *'heaving-to'* may not be much different. This consists of hauling the storm jib to weather, the trysail amidships and the lashing the tiller to leeward (or wheel to windward). (Fig 6.12). This is a passive tactic: the alternative is to keep the boat moving. The reason for movement is that the rudder can operate and control the boat. Having no way on, of course, means no results from rudder movement. So we will try to what is called *'fore-reach'* . This is only one removed from hove-to, but the storm jib is allowed to fill normally and the boat begins to sail forward. It must *not be fast* . No one is saying that you should try and beat to windward against the storm. This is an important reason for having a *small* storm jib (and small trysail). The tactic is as follows. The yacht is sailed between 60 and 90 degrees to the apparent wind (Fig 6.13). As the approach of a steep breaking sea, the boat is shot almost right into the wind. She does this with the previous momentum and the instant the crest

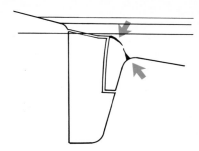

Fig 6.11 Rudder skegs may be a potential menace in severe conditions.

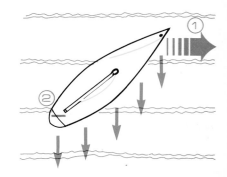

Fig 6.12 Traditional method of 'heaving-to'. At times boat may make way forward (1), but can be thrown back on her rudder (2).

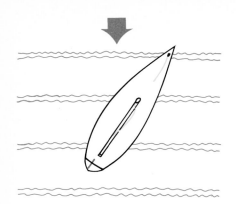

Fig 6.13 The modern 'fore-reach'. Sailing slow and close to the wind with very small area and a man at the helm...

into the cockpit. It also means that the yacht will sail down into the trough between the seas rather than get carried along in a surfing crest which is fraught with danger. The yacht may surf for anything up to half a mile and control could be lost if the rudder is in foam rather than relatively solid water. Some authorities say that the 'correct speed' is all important (this speed and control factor again!): too fast causes surfing, but too slow results in taking heavy water or pitch poling. If the yacht takes the crest at too great an angle, (Fig 6.15) she will in effect be nearly broadside on, in other words, broaching and a-hull and a knock down, followed possibly by a capsize (inversion) can follow. (Fig 6.16). Speed can also be lost

Fig 6.14 ...with the modern yacht this is the intended effect, meeting a crest almost head on, then bearing away to get moving again.

of the sea is surmounted, the helm is put up (wheel down) and she cuts away through the breaking crest, once more at 60-90 degrees. (Fig 6.13).

Compare this with being hove-to with no steerable course. (Fig 6.12). Then the yacht can be flung aft on to her rudder. If you think about it she is kind of running down wind and sea stern first. It is a nasty feeling, I can tell you. She may end up damaging her steering gear, filling the cockpit or lying a-hull for the next huge sea to knock her down.

To return to the fore reaching boat, the act of putting the helm down (or wheel up) has to be *positive and relatively late* as the big crest gets near. It is the sail power just before putting the helm down which is the key speed in this tactic. It is not the lower half of the sea which is the problem, but the top third, which has the breaking crest. The sheets are not trimmed; there is no time and the howling conditions do not allow it. The pulling away from the crest *must be quick* : do not stall or get stuck head to wind. By bearing off it will also stop dropping down on to an intermediate sea with a horrible bang.

If all this sounds exhausting remember that the action is not on every wave: it is only on those which are breaking heavily. This tactic is not recommended for older heavy boats that are slow to respond to the helm. It is for moderate and light displacement fast cruisers. (Fig 6.14)

The other main option is to keep moving, but essentially *down wind* . Obviously adequate sea room is essential: the 40 ft (12.2 m) boat may be 100 miles to leeward after 13 to 14 hours. For the force 9 or above and especially in force 10 or 11, no sail is required to keep good steerage way off the wind. Bare pole, even with the low windage modern spar, is enough. Try this out in a strong wind one day, whether in the open sea or sheltered water. Of course, storm sails must be ready in order to sail up or fore reach, if necessary at any moment. (e.g. man overboard or to avoid another vessel). Some ocean sailors would leave the storm jib aloft even in extreme conditions but sheeted hard in using both sheets. The yacht is then steered, but at a fine angle to the advancing seas. If large breakers are taken fine on the quarter, they are less likely to break

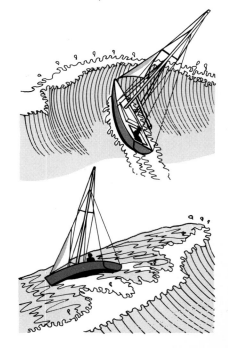

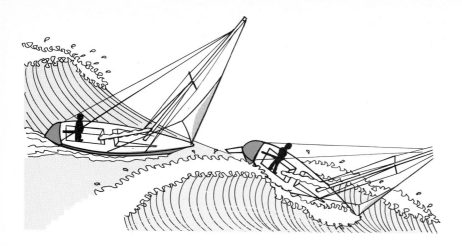

dangerously in a trough due to being blanketed by the next sea! This applies in very big waves and it sounds like the storm jib would help here.

The major variation in these kind of tactics is to *stream or tow a big warp* astern. In such conditions any work on deck is very laborious with the crew hanging on and moving slowly. Heavy spray sweeps across them and the wind claws at them. There must be an argument for fetching a warp and paying it out astern. The classic reason is to slow the yacht down to stop surfing, for instance. It is also said, if payed out in a large bight with an end secured on each quarter to 'quieten the sea' and reduce the tendency of a crest to break. It may also 'hold the stern' on to the seas, where otherwise the rudder may leave solid water and control be lost. (Fig 6.17). Experienced views are conflicting. Frank Mulville, who has crossed the Atlantic a number of times says 'the effect is remarkable - a narrow path will form immediately where the seas only occasionally break and surfing will cease although the odd crest may

still break aboard.' Robin Knox-Johnston in very big seas in the southern ocean streamed a big bight of floating warp with small storm jib sheeted hard and helm lashed. Moitessier said that his boat was saved, when he decided to cut his trailing warps. They were however very heavy and had netting and ballast on!

Fig 6.16 Whether sailing into the wind or running, getting side on to the crest can result in this.

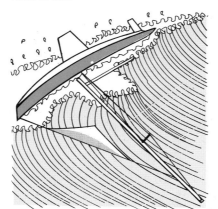

For the fast cruiser, if the skipper has decided that the time has come to run before the storm and if he has no special preference or experience, then, the storm sails securely lashed, run off with the best helmsman at the tiller or wheel and no sail set. Have a big floating (if possible) warp ready of between 40 fathoms (73 m) and

Fig 6.17 Warps trailed from the stern may aid riding to huge seas.

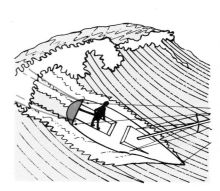

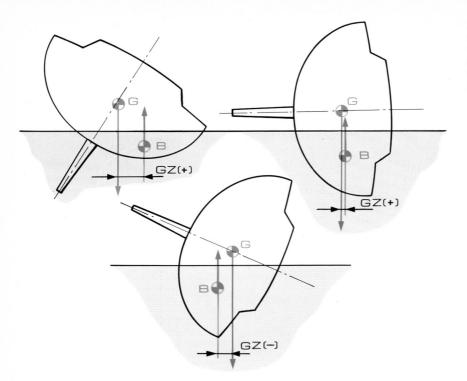

Fig 6.18 Basics of yacht stability. GZ is the righting arm, determined at any instant by G, the centre of gravity (fixed) and B the centre of buoyancy. Note small GZ at knock down and negative GZ when beyond horizontal (in the case of this yacht).

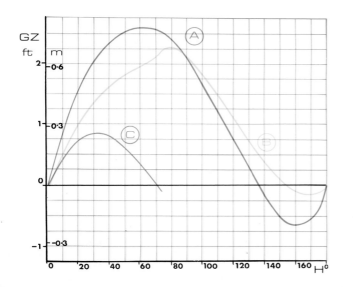

Fig 6.19 These are GZ curves. A is a modern high freeboard fin keel sloop. B is a moderately long keel low freeboard sloop and C is a Danish fishing vessel. GZ is the righting at various angles of keel and becomes negative very early for the fishing vessel; at about 140 degrees for A and at 150 degrees for B. The latter only has a small negative righting arm when inverted. Yachts of different types will show widely varying GZ curves. Remember these represent static stability.

100 fathoms (183 m), but do not use it initially. Steer a course between stern dead to sea and 20 degrees, taking breaking crests as described above. These are then variables to try out to regulate speed and boat behaviour, namely the storm jib, the trysail and the warp or warps.

Stability

If any yacht can be knocked down, does it matter what shape is the hull and how the whole vessel is designed in terms of its weight distribution, its centre of gravity and shape of deck structure? Yes, it does because on these factors depend the recovery from the knock down and whether the yacht will roll over or become inverted and stay like that – a shocking experience, but which has occurred in storm conditions.

An 'ordinary' ballasted yacht behaves as in Fig. 6.18 at various angles of heel and extreme angles. As a yacht begins to heel the righting arm (GZ) increases all the time and this is the usual feeling that the crew get in ordinary close hauled sailing. However by the time the yacht is hove down with the mast parallel with the water – knocked down – then although the righting arm is still very great it is actually decreasing in quantity as the boat is hove down yet further. Boats other than ballasted yachts behave quite differently; multihulls have a negative righting arm when nearly horizontal which never returns and, in the example, a Danish fishing vessel (upon which tests were made) loses all stability at 70 degrees, but she should never get near such an angle. (Fig 6.19).

What the yacht curves show are that an angle of heel often somewhere around 130 degrees from the vertical, the stability becomes negative and the yacht will go on until she is floating with the keel vertically upwards. Between about 70 degrees and this 130, she is struggling to recover, and would do so if there were no external forces (a breaking wave for instance!), but if the vessel is being pushed in some way then its righting arm is decreasing all the time. But the stability curves vary from design to design and the owner is interested in the characteristics that give good or bad curves. A low centre of gravity, which means low ballast and plenty of it compared with the rest of the weight in the yacht is obviously useful. A cross section of hull with a particularly large beam will increase the negative righting arm when this applies (a wide plank is stable either way up). (Fig 6.20). A big coachroof (cabin trunk) reduces the negative righting arm (Fig 6.21), since when it is immersed it gives buoyancy against further heeling. In theory at any rate the big trunk makes the centre of gravity higher, so it does not help until it is immersed (which we never want to happen). High freeboard comes into the same category.

In the incidents recorded of yachts

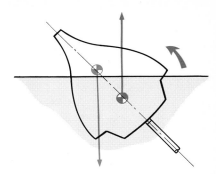

Fig 6.2! A narrow hull and the addition of a coach roof help prevent inverted stability.

being turned completely over, on many occasions they appear to have continued their roll, coming up the other side, but some have stayed upside down for several minutes. Something then is needed to move them on. This might be the weight of all the crew placed against one side inside the hull, or a further wave crest striking the keel (Fig 6.22). This brings us to the difference between static and dynamic stability, which is not just theory, but an important point to making sure that a fast

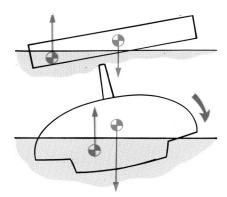

Fig 6.20 A reminder that very large beam tends to make a yacht stable when inverted – a flat plank also!

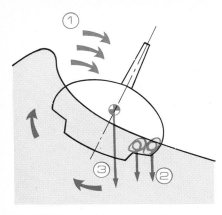

Fig 6.22 How yachts can return from a knock down regardless of theoretical inverted stability. 1 is moving or breaking crest. 2 is crew weight. 3 is yacht's own centre of gravity.

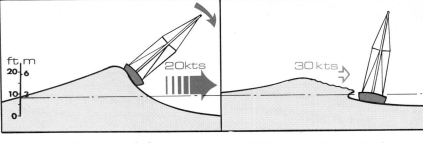

Fig 6.24 Two waves about to break on a yacht. The first is frame B in 6.23 which will break half a second later. It is moving at 20 knots; the second is frame E where an already broken crest is travelling at 30 knots.

cruiser can be trusted in severe weather. What we have just been talking about is static theory and practice – what a yacht would do in flat water. Here the facts are known and tested; they can be tested in harbour and in the tank. Dynamic stability is less well understood. How do we know *exactly* what happens as all is suddenly darkness and ones world is thrown on its side or upside down? If we do not know then we cannot reproduce controlled conditions, even if it was simple to do so. Knowledge continues to be acquired; yacht designers and researchers are concerned.

As the storm blows, seas build in a random fashion and, among the waves of all sizes, are some much steeper than a 'regular' wave. The forward face is steep enough for a crest to form. The breaking crest has a speed greater than that of the wave. How the wave may thus break is shown in Fig 6.23. Much depends emphasizes that the normal static

at what stage in its break, the crest meets the yacht. In Fig 6.24 two stages of these crests may roll the boat near horizontal or even beyond. At such a stage tons of water moving forward lifts the boat bodily sideways in the accelerating breaking sea rushing down its own wave form. D.J. Jordan of Massachusetts Institute of Technology has researched this theory with models and he emphasizes that the normal static forces have little effect. The breaking sea was found to strike a 30 ft (9 m) yacht and move her to leeward at 13 knots and roll her at 60 degrees per second. This is equivalent to crew hearing and seeing a kind of waterfall ('suddenly we saw this enormous breaking sea') and then seconds later everything happening too quick to take in. In these tests boat size was found to be related to sea size. A breaking wave of at least 20 ft (6 m) was needed to capsize a 30 ft (9 m) boat and a 40 ft (12.2 m) wave to capsize a 60 ft (24.5 m) boat. The force on the larger yacht would be eight times that on the smaller.

Using these dynamic tests, Jordan

Fig 6.23 Representation of a deep water breaking wave (after Jordan). One half a second between each frame. Dimensions in feet and metres.

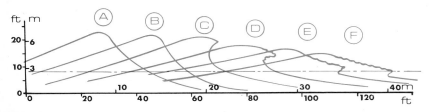

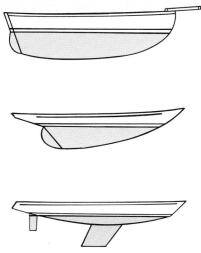

Fig 6.25 These three yacht types were all found to behave in much the same way in a knock down. A long keel boat (1927 design), a 1950s ocean racer and 1980s ocean racer. However recovery may be a different matter (e.g. Figs 6.18 - 6.21).

6.3 Fog!

also found out something about design features which made a yacht vulnerable to knock down and possible capsize. Light displacement for a given size made a boat accelerate faster when hit by the crest and more likely to damage. Freeboard increased the area which could be hit by the crest; compare this with its help if and when immersed, but its contribution to high centre of gravity. A fin keel was slightly better than a long keel, because the latter tended to 'trip up' the yacht, but the difference was not great. Large beam was not found to have any effect one way or the other. In the tests three very different known designs were used, one very long keel boat from the year 1927, a typical 1950 offshore racer with a long keel though slightly cut away forward and a modern (1981) ocean racer. (Fig 6.25). No one boat had any special resistance to knock down: this seems to agree (earlier this chapter) with the known facts that knock downs have happened to widely different yachts in various parts of the world.

The Jordan tests were dynamic, but remember that once the knock down has happened and it is followed by a partial or full capsize and perhaps a total inversion, then despite the broken water and moving waves, the yacht is bound to obey largely the principles of static stability just reviewed above. (e.g. Figs 6.18 - 6.21).

Fog

Sooner or later the fast cruiser will meet fog, often considered as perilous as heavy weather. However it is not unrelenting in the same way as a gale: there is often a calm sea, light wind and actual enjoyment in navigating through it successfully, as an expected or at least a recognized mark appears out of the gloom. The sound of fog signals is even nostalgic, one of those sea sounds that some come to associate with life on board. (P 6.3).

When visibility deteriorates to 1 km or about half a nautical mile, fog is said to exist. There are various causes, some prevalent in particular

parts of the world combined with season, so local sailing directions should be consulted. Whatever the original cause, fog is made of minute invisible droplets into which water vapour, usually present invisibly in the air has condensed. This air has cooled by being in contact with the sea surface at a low temperature. The causes of fog at sea are described as follows. *Sea fog, or advection fog* is associated with moist relatively warm air flowing over a cold sea surface. It is the main fog experienced at sea. It is most common in late spring and early summer when sea temperature is lowest compared with air temperature. Where there are cold currents such as off Newfoundland and New England and off California such fogs can happen at any time. The Labrador current in conjunction with moist air from S or SW gives an average of 10 days per month fog.

Frontal fog occurs on a warm front or advancing depression. It happens in temperate and cold climates (Fig 6.26) and is caused by warm rain

85

Fig 6.27 Fog strategy and tactics (with acknowledgements to Professor Brian Lacey.

FOG STRATEGY AND TACTICS

drops falling on cold air beneath the front. It will not last long, but strong winds around the depression may follow.

Radiation fog is fine weather fog. The land cools on a clear night and fog forms over it late in the night and persists into the early morning. It may be most frequent over low lying marshy country, or where there is industrial pollution. It drifts out to sea, but seldom more than 10 miles offshore by which time it has thinned out completely. 15 miles offshore would be a maximum.

Arctic sea smoke, or frost smoke is found in high latitudes only, where few yachts sail. Very cold air from ice or snow causes intense evaporation from a relatively warm sea. This moisture is immediately chilled and forms fog, which gives the sea the appearance of steaming.

Warnings of fog may come over weather forecasts, but whether you run into one of the patches expected is a matter of chance. Fog can be forecast by observation. If sea temperature converges with the dew point, fog will probably form. If a yacht does not carry such equipment, or the crew are too busy to engage in such work, then it is a question of being ready to cope with fog whenever it comes.

Fog can creep up quite suddenly. At night it may be some time before the watch on deck realizes that the visibility has gone, perhaps by disappearance of his own or other vessel's lights. If there is some warning, then it may be possible to modify plans to avoid passage among rocks or sandbanks, areas of tricky tide or current

Before cruising

A compass of known deviation, a dependable RDF set with up-to-date details of beacons, a depth meter (with lead-line for back up), and up-to-date large scale charts, light lists and tide tables are obviously of most importance in boats without radar. An efficient radar reflector and radar emission detector have an importance in proportion to the local density of shipping. A log. VHF radio, list of VHF lighthouses, fog horn and quiet engine are also clearly desirable though of comparatively small value. For the lone deaf sailor a working hearing-aid could be vital.

When cruising

A wise sailor will always 'log, lead and lookout', keep up a reasonable DR position, record weather forecasts, keep the engine in a state to start instantly and work up tidal streams and depths in good time before landfall.

When fog is forecast or predicted

The sailing plan should be modified as necessary to avoid as far as possible passage among rocks, reefs or sandbanks (particularly with cross currents), races, overfalls or traffic lanes where fair visibility is necessary for safe navigation. Make sure batteries are fully charged for Loran C, Decca and electronic aids; also for immediate engine start in emergency.

As visibility is seen to deteriorate

The pros and cons of all available options should be weighed-up at once. If already among immediate dangers (mentioned above) the choice of options must be made urgently. Alternatively a safe interval for thought must be created by marking-time at once if away form shipping or diverting to do so, ideally into water too shallow for big ships, if not. The position of the boat should be fixed as well as possible and the position and course of other boats and the position of visible hazards noted while there is still sufficient visibility.

Tactics in fog

a) Make at once towards any buoy or seamark that can be safely approached, while it is still visible or audible, especially if the identity of the mark or the direction or speed of tidal stream is uncertain.

b) Switch on radar emission monitor, and of course radar, if possessed.

c) Check depth and keep under continual review.

d) Put up radar reflector if not already raised.

e) Listen continually while sailing. Switch off engine at short intervals to listen for fog signals, ships engines, breakers, tide rips etc.

f) Sound own fog horn only if other small boats are known or thought likely to be near.

g) Don't stare into the fog. Scan the whole horizon at two-minute intervals.

h) Get an anchor ready if near shallows

or reefs particularly if in an area of fast tidal streams or cross currents and most particularly if with no engine and no wind.

i) Sail as long as there is wind but check that the engine is instantaneously startable.

j) If a radar emission detector is possessed: scan all the horizon at intervals suitable to the known or expected density of traffic or detected emission.

k) Estimate the visibility from the speed and time taken for a buoy or other seamark to disappear.

l) At night, take care to maintain dark adaptation and keep a powerful spotlight (eg. 50-100 watt quartz-iodine) to hand as usual: to shine, if need be, directly at a ship's bridge, signal D in Morse (I am manoeuvering with difficulty, keep clear), or read the name or pick up reflective or fluorescent paint on an unlit buoy or other mark.

m) When close-hauled, sail a definite course, rather than full-and-by, in order to keep a better DR.

n) Check all relevant tidal streams, height of water, fog and light signals and obstructions near course.

o) Log everything and keep the DR position continually updated with a realistic circle of uncertainty.

p) Get life jackets ready and check readiness of liferaft and inflatable if unavoidably in heavy traffic.

q) Use any available beacon or VHF lighthouse to home on, fix position or monitor progress.

r) Home on a beacon with circumspection and bring on the better bow in good time.

s) Do not steer directly towards a fog signal or light: keep it fine on the better bow.

t) Bear in mind the relatively short range of fog signals when running down wind and on hot summer days.

u) Consider the possibility of getting above the fog or improving the audibility of fog signals by going aloft.

v) If you fail to find a silent seamark at the expected time and place, search for it by sailing or motoring about its presumed position along the perimeter of a square whose sides are at first equal to twice the visibility, then four times and perhaps a third time with sides of eight times the visibility.

w) Approach shallow and shores at an angle of 30°, rather than 90°, whenever possible.

Strategy in fog

It is reassuring to realize that in fog, as in other hazardous situations in sailing, one is never obliged to stick to one course of action since there are always alternatives. In general however the choices are restricted to seven, not all of which will be available in every instance:

a) continue sailing toward the original destination.

b) substitute a new destination and alter course accordingly.

c) mark-time at once by anchoring, **heaving-to or motoring or jilling to and fro**, roughly beam-on to the wind, to and from a known position or seamark.

d) divert to a place suitable for marking time as in c) above – eg, by heading out to sea or into shallow water with wind offshore.

e) follow (or possibly accept a tow from) another boat to an agreed destination or a safe position.

f) head back towards the starting point.

g) seek help by radio.

Factors affecting choice of action

The factors to be considered can be classified as follows:

a) Quality and comprehensiveness of the yacht's fog equipment including radar emission detection. With electronic position finding aids, with high reliability shown on the instrument, many of the navigational tactics above will become ancillary.

b) Reliability of the yacht's position at the relevant time.

c) Presence of hazards, particularly shipping, between yacht and possible destinations.

d) Comparative ease of maintenance of position on way to destinations.

e) Ease of access to a safe place to mark time.

f) Density and expected extent and duration of fog judged by its presumed nature, time of day, forecasts etc.

g) Comparative ease of entrance to harbour and safe anchorage at all possible destinations.

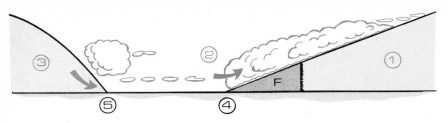

Fig 6.26 Section through a depression, showing where fog (and wind) are met. 1 is cool air. F is fog where 'warm' rain meets cold air and wind is increasing. 2 is warm air. 3 is cold air. 4 is warm front. 5 is cold front.

and shipping lanes. The position should be fixed, even when there are electronic position finding instruments - after all once the fog comes down they are the only fix. If there is a buoy or other mark near when the fog is about to close in, then sail up to it to check the stream or current.

Tactics and strategy in fog are listed in the table (Fig 6.27). Such a comprehensive list may make you wonder whether you should ever leave harbour in fog. Why not? It is easier to leave in bad visibility than to arrive. Of course, it depends on the features met leaving harbour (heavy shipping or fishing area, difficult currents etc), but, for instance radiation fog may be thicker in harbour than outside. The sun may be blazing down 10 miles out. Similarly frontal fog is short lived. When fast cruising it may pay to leave in fog and a few hours later, as a successful passage is being enjoyed, it may be forgotten, or even better notched up as another challenge competently overcome.

The successful outcome of an encounter with tough conditions or other undesirable happenings at sea such as man overboard, fire, collision, gear breakage or personal injury depends tremendously on preparation. Preparation means attention to detail and detail has nothing to do with triviality. Scores of rightly prepared items provide the ability to cope when things go wrong and confidence at sea when they are going well. The author makes no secret of being a 'belt and braces (suspenders) man', but that does not involve cluttering the fast cruiser with heavy spares.

After taking delivery of a new yacht in early 1979, I noticed among other things that the swinging stove was stopped by joinery after it reached an angle outboard of about 40 degrees. Its pivots, though strong, were open so that it could be lifted out easily. Quickly I drilled holes through the pivot recesses and in-serted heavy split pins (cotter pins) so the stove could not jump out. In August 1979, several boats of the same type caught like mine in the Fastnet storm, suffered serious damage and crew injury from the heavy stove crashing across the saloon. The combination of the obstruction to swing at any angle and the lack of pivot locks was very dangerous indeed. Those two split pins were a detail, but a very important one.

Of the important details listed here some are based on international safety regulations for ocean racing. They are actually the 'special regulations of the international Offshore Racing Council', so that they represent a systemized list built up after wide experience and approved by the representatives of all countries. On the debit side it means that they tend to be a lowest common denominator - what 'everyone can be got to agree'. Anyway they are designed as '*minimum* equipment and accommodations standards'. So they do not cover everything (what does ?), yet some cruising skippers might consider a boat equipped to such standards was exceptionally and rather expensively organized. Of course, one man will insist on carrying item A, while another says A is superfluous and he would spend the money on B. So no one will agree with the exact scale of the equipment I mention. The ORC regulations will be considered later in this section, but first let us look at a basic check list for the fast cruiser.

Hull and deck check list

Classification societies (official surveyors) will issue certificates in various countries after supervising the building of individual or production yachts. Such societies are Lloyds Register, the American Bureau of Shipping and Bureau Veritas. The American Bureau of

7.1 International safety rules, scantlings by ABS and useful British and Irish handicap systems for cruisers.

Fig 7.1 Hull and deck check list for trouble free cruising. Many of these points should be incorporated in building or converting. Otherwise modifications must be made.

Shipping in conjunction with the ORC has issued a 'Guide for building and classing offshore racing yachts' (P 7.1). My belief is that few racing boat designers (in their efforts to keep one jump ahead and forever light in weight) bother with it, but it is a sound guide for fast cruisers. Its 57 pages and (at any moment) its latest amendments cover building materials and their control, fastenings, plating in aluminium, glass reinforced plastics, steel and wood in various forms, frames and stiffening, rudders and rudder stocks (in some detail) and hatches and windows (very sketchily).

My hull, deck and rig list is tabulated in Fig 7.1. They are design and fitting out matters. Among these listed it is worth emphasizing a few points. For *bilge drainage* a sump in

the top of the keel is a comforting thing. Without this in a modern flat bilge, fin keel design, the smallest amount of water is a curse (Fig 7.2). The owner or skipper should have a knowledge of how every part of the *steering gear* works (Fig 7.3), which has been obtained from the builder (he may have altered the designer's intention in small working details). Then if noises, vibrations or other difficulties develop, someone on board will be able to make a competent investigation and then, if necessary make plans for putting any trouble right. The notes and sketches show the fitting of the bearings, how the stock is attached to the blade, what stops the stock falling out of the boat, what keeps the tiller tight to the stock and so on. Conditions at sea may well be bad when such memo

is consulted, or the yacht may be in an isolated foreign harbour far from yacht-yard facilities and know-how.

Interior liners are dangerous in the event of a leak. The average boat show is full of awful examples of liners blocking off access (P 7.2), which the builder shows you proudly. One yacht had a knock down and shipped much water: the crew thought they had a serious leak for some time afterwards and were highly distressed until it was found that the water was steadily pouring out of all the interior liners.

Switches for the engine, including the ignition switch and start button should be below out of the wet; the cockpit of a seagoing boat is not the place for them. The only control in the cockpit should be the combined throttle/gear lever to the engine and

Fig 7.2 A bilge sump in the keel, if it can be arranged, prevents small amounts of water spreading in modern shallow bilge yachts. The end of the bilge pump should be led into it.

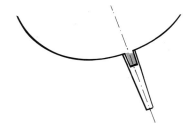

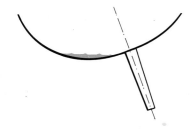

LIST OF DESIGN AND FITTING OUT POINTS

This list of design and fitting out points is mostly based on a list originally collected by Roderick Stephens.

Hull

1. *Steering* must be free and firm without stiffness or backslash. It is worth persisting in yardwork until this is completely right.
2. *Bilge drainage.* A tea cup of water poured in anywhere must find its way fairly quickly to the lowest part of the bilge, whence it can be pumped out.
3. Permanent *flotation marks* on centreline fore and aft on the datum waterline and a further set twelve inches above them are useful for checking the trim at any time.
4. Propeller *shaft marking* should be provided so that the propeller can be turned to minimum resistance from inside the yacht before a race begins.
5. The propeller *shaft lock* should be a sheer pin (brass) which will lock for normal use but can be severed in an emergency. Brake systems not fully released can create a fire hazard.
6. There should be *no sharp edges* or corners in the accommodation or on deck.
7. *Bilges* with a rough finish are almost impossible to keep clean.
8. Impenetrable *interior liners* are too common in GRP boats and must be avoided.
9. *Electric switches* should be sited clear of water and spray. I is better to have to reach a bit further and have the switches work.
10. The *emergency tiller* should be fitted form time to time (swollen wood?, rusted steel?) Does it affect the compass? A strong person should then treat it very roughly, as a test!
11. *Cockpit drain guard* should be a light gauge cross, which stops potential blocking objects getting down, but offers no measurable obstruction to quick water outflow. The same applies to diaphragm pump intakes.
12. *Through hull fittings.* Sinks must not be sited low so that they take in water when heeled. *Water intakes* (toilet etc.) must be low so that they operate when heeled. The *exhaust for the engine* must be well above the waterline even when down by the stern when motoring fast, running in a seaway or heeled. *Seacocks* must be fitted on all skin fittings, be reasonable of access, turned easily by hand and marked in the 'full open' and 'full shut' positions. The *bilge pump discharge* should not be an *inward* source of water: the pipe should be looped high under the deck and discharge above the waterline on or near the centreline. *Fuel tank vents* should be on or near the centreline where fumes cannot be carried into the accommodation. *Water tank vents* should emerge at a sink or drain below decks where overflow when filling does not matter, yet there is no chance of salt water contamination.

Deck and rig

1. *Sail tyers and small lines.* Plenty of these are always useful and they should be kept in marked or coloured bags which are readily accessible.
2. *Goosenecks* and kicking straps are frequently blocked by gear or fittings when the boom is squared off which can result in dangerous strains: clearance must be made where necessary.
3. *Split pins.* The pin should be cut so that below the head it is one and a half times the diameter of the clevis pin which is being secured. The ends, after cutting, shoud be rounded with a smooth flat file. If possible in use they should be slightly opened and not bent right back: however, depending on the fitting this may be necessary so that tape can be applied smoothly to prevent fouling. All exposed split pins should be taped everywhere on deck or in the rig. (*Cotter pin* US.)
4. *Bitter ends.* All halyards should be arranged so they can never go aloft. Ends can be tied, shackled, or stopper knots, large enough not to enter blocks or mast sheaves, made in their ends.
5. *Mast wiring.* Wiring to navigation lights on pulpits or mast should not use so-called waterproof plugs. Wires should pass through the deck and then connect to main supply

below deck as high up as possible. Where a mast is stepped to the keel, wiring is sometimes damaged when the mast is unstepped. A good arrangement is a longitudinal hole that permits disconnected wires to be lodged inside when the mast is being moved. These wires are fished out when required to be connected and taken to their various hook-up points (not close to the mast partners).

6. *Lubrication.* An oil can should be kept within reach and used frequently on all moving gear (spinnaker pistons, goose neck track, metal cam jammers, snap shackles etc.) on deck. Otherwise salt water will jam many fittings tight.

7. *Boatswain's chair.* A boat that does not carry one cannot expect to repair or adjust anything more than about ten feet above the deck. You might as well have the engine compartment sealed in a power boat! The strops must be short, so that when the chair shackle is two blocks, the man aloft is within reach of the masthead. The hoist should have a metal ring of such gauge that it will take any halyard shackle in use. The seat should be smooth but not varnished and, as is well known, the strops must be spliced below it, so that if it breaks the user is still supported by them.

8. *Halyard noise.* It must be possible despite leads and splices, for all halyards to be taken clear of the mast and still be secured, so that they will not tap the mast when the boat is left in her berth.

9. *Storm jib.* This must have been hoisted, sheeted and lowered, preferably in a good breeze which will show any defects in its function. The deck is usually laid out ideally for genoas, but sometimes difficulties can arise with jibs. This is particularly so for (a) *effective deck leads,* (snatch blocks can burst open, does the jib lead inside the shrouds, or outside like a genoa?), (b) *head spans* (are there extra pieces to fit a groove?), (c) *emergency hanking* by lacing when the groove is not usable and (d) whether *special sheets* should be available (genoa sheets are unnecessarily long for jibs).

10. As well as checking all the small components in the rig by sending a knowledgable person aloft to examine all parts of the mast, spreaders and rigging, the line should be followed via chain plates to tie bars into the hull. Examine fastenings in wood, welds in steel and alloy and glassing in, however designed, in plastics (glass, kevlar and other synthetic reinforced plastics, polyester, epoxys, vinylester etc). Look for hair line cracks, movement evidenced by dirt lines or corrosion.

11. If there is a *fin keel,* is there any sign of stress where it meets the hull such as hairline cracks or displaced filler? If there has been a heavy grounding, such inspection should be repeated with the boat ashore, even if there is no apparent defect when afloat after the incident.

this must be recessed to avoid fouling lines or getting damaged in any way. Stripping down a *seacock* is one of the few jobs that cannot be done afloat (even a propeller can be inspected by lifting the stern). A seacock that has been stripped, cleaned and greased with seacock grease will perform for a couple of seasons. (Fig 7.4). *Split pins* (cotter pins) should be kept in all sizes as spares in a plastic box which can be found instantly. The same box also contains small components; unless in very good conditions do not reuse split pins. Small key ring type pins, with which a number of clevis pins come equipped have no place at sea. Replace them with split pins. They can be torn open or wind themselves out. (P 7.3)

7.2 Neat moulded liners, but do they block off access?

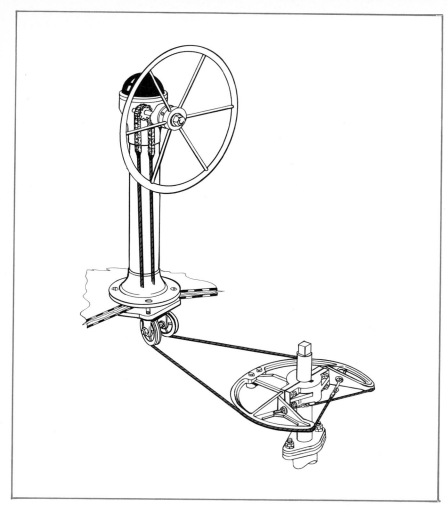

7.3 Very small, but important. Split (cotter) pins, seizing wire, wood bung, clevis pin and for winches, pawls, pawl-springs, circlip and Allen key.

Fig 7.4 Typical of the fittings that are easily stripped down by owner and crew. The bronze seacock which once a year should be taken apart and greased. The result: easy working and no leaking.

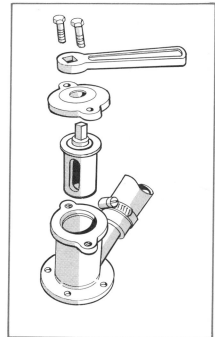

If all the small irritations and defects which occur in the normal cruising mileage are going to be put right, then they must be listed as soon as they are noticed. If this is not done, then they will be overlooked for sure when the boat is back in harbour. The best plan is to write the defect straight into the log book when it is in use sailing; then extract as a list at the end of the passage.

Fig 7.3 Owner's plan of his wheel steering, so that if problems arise, he can tackle any part of the mechanism.

Drills at sea and in harbour

It is no use having all the listed right equipment if it does not work or more likely has never been — as far as possible — tested. The ORC regulations express this as well as anywhere. They say: all required equipment shall (a) function properly, (b) be readily accessible and (c) be of types, sizes and capacities suitable and adequate for the intended use and size of the yacht. It is possible to categorize most equipment into either regular gear or emergency gear. The liferaft is obviously in the former category, harnesses are in the latter. I do not like the word 'safety', here since the whole concept of boat gear and crew should provide safety and having particular pieces of equipment does not make the yacht safe.

In regular sailing, there are certain times that demand drills. Action as fog closes down has already been mentioned; so has the routine as heavy weather approaches. In addition to these, regular drills are useful before *leaving harbour,* on *return to harbour* at the end of a short cruise, before *nightfall.* Emergency drills should be available for *man overboard* and in case of *impact damage.*

Before leaving harbour on a cruise of any length there seem to be a thousand things to be done. Every skipper will have his own lists and it would be pointless to show every possibility here. Among obvious points are stocking up with freshwater including freshly filled spare cans in case a main supply has leaked. Use water tank pills (e.g. 'Aquatabs') to ensure containers and lines remain clean. Fuel for motor. Fuel for cooking stove (gas, paraffin (kerosene), or spirit (alcohol)). Food and ice. Batteries fully charged (test with hydrometer). The navigator must check out his department especially charts and sailing directions for the intended area with latest corrections. If the skipper is doing this as well, he must allow plenty of time. Sometimes

7.4 Marks on the shaft will prevent sailing with a folding propeller partly open.

charts are not immediately available, so planning for these may be weeks before rather than days.

It is important to check that all defects listed from a previous cruise are rectified *and tested.* Don't trust third party's reporting that the job has been done. I have hoisted sails, which had been repaired only to find that one fault had been corrected, but not all! Anyway are all sails taken ashore for repair back on board – or anything else that was taken ashore? Each member of the crew must look after his own bedding, clothing and personal effects, but in the event of anyone inexperienced the skipper should check. Proper foul weather gear and boots? Thermal underwear or other method of keeping warm? For hot weather sun burn lotion and also pills for headaches and sea sickness? Individuals should have their own supplies because although they are in the yacht's first aid kit, it is not reasonable to have continual demands on it.

Other points on or soon after leaving harbour are: ensure all moving parts on deck are lubricated – a touch of light oil does wonders in a salt climate; check all electrics and electronics are operating. Once the boat is moving and before she reaches the open sea: lower log impeller and check it appears to be reading correctly (otherwise clear weed from it); check all running rigging is properly led on deck (it may not have been possible to arrange this while mooring lines were in position); go below when motor has been stopped and line up folding propeller on mark already on shaft; (P 7.4) for feathering propeller fix blades fore and aft; final check on stowage of everything below and bilge drained dry.

On return to harbour

This requires more of a check, for after all when you are putting to sea, the crew is on board and can put things right later if not sooner. When the boat is left until next weekend or a few weeks, then a check list is the only way of ensuring jobs are done. A typical list is shown in Fig 7.5 and everyone will amend and add items for himself. And always when leaving the boat, it will be MAIN BATTERY SWITCHES OFF, SEACOCKS SHUT (except engine cooling water inlet), VENTILATORS OPEN, BILGE DRY and HATCHES AND COMPANIONWAYS LOCKED.

Impact damage. After hitting a rock or other obstruction, the

Fig 7.5 A check list on return to harbour. Go through this then everything will be ready for he next weekend or cruising period.

Has defect list from log book been transferred to a list for use on shore?
Did the boat touch bottom at any time or was any damage inflicted that might require attention?
Is all the running rigging – sheets, guys and halyards – free of chafe? Were any sails torn or damaged in any way that might require attention?
Is the bottom clean enough for the next outing or will it need scrubbing?
Is the standing rigging properly set up – correct shroud tension, etc?
Are all the terminal fittings operable, snap shackles properly lubricated etc?
Are all the winches and turning blocks operable? Do they require stripping and lubricating?
Was any item of equipment lost or broken that might require replacing – winch handles, snatch blocks etc?
Do the batteries require changing? Are all the navigation lights, instruments and cabin light functioning?
Do the charts require drying out? Are the correct charts aboard for the next race?
Is there adequate fuel and water aboard?
Has the crew been informed of the arrangements? Has any food that will not stay fresh been cleared out? Have food and refreshment arrangements been made? If any chores have to be carried out by the crew do they have the full information they require?
Do the sails require drying out?
Has the backstay been eased off?
Are all the ventilators open?
Have the log impellers been retracted?
Are the bilges dry?
Have the seacocks and isolating power switches been turned off?
Are all hatches and companionways and ports locked for security?

following is the recommended drill. Reduce speed or stop by reducing sail, so long as the yacht's position permits. Later it may be necessary to anchor, again depending on the position. Issue life-jackets to all the crew. Raise cabin sole and check if the yacht is making water. If there is no inflow check for damage to steering, propeller shaft (turn it slowly from inside), speedo impellers and other skin fittings.

If there is inflow, get tools, softwood plugs (see ORC rule 6.52) and repair materials clear of bilge. Switch on RT for transmission of distress call (MAYDAY) if necessary later. Make ready but do not yet launch life-raft. Part of the crew then endeavour to repair damage, while others prepare for abandonment, get visual signals ready, or steer boat towards shallow water.

Man overboard. (Fig 7.6). Prevention is better than cure and every device mentioned in this book – harnesses, non-slip deck, handholds, cockpit design and other precautions – should be taken to avoid this unnerving occurance. Various drills are taught and experienced sailors know that in the event there are numerous ways of picking up a person from the water,

depending on the yacht, conditions, strength of crew left on board and so on. Several methods are recommended and will be found in *This is Rough Weather Sailing* page 120 by Erroll Bruce (in this series). Without in any way claiming that one system is better than another, here is a drill which should certainly be given consideration.

The boat may be close-hauled, reaching or running, but (1) as soon as the man has gone overboard put the boat on a reach with apparent wind just on the beam (2) at the same time drop lifebuoy, marker etc. (3) One man watches the person in the water, or (second best) the marker which has been dropped near him; all the crew on deck, of course. Another person watches the compass course. (4) After sailing about one cable (200 m), harden up quickly, tack and come on to the other reach with wind still abeam; the apparent wind (A) will therefore still be slightly ahead of the beam (5). The yacht should now be heading

Fig 7.6 Picking up a man overboard depends on the circumstances and a single drill cannot be insisted on. This shows a method recommended in the adjoining text.

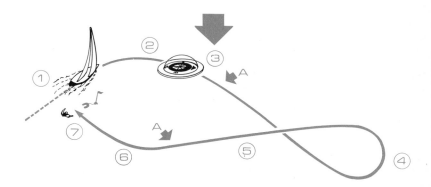

straight back towards the man and the compass course reciprocal from the previous one.

Once the yacht is near the man in the water, the problem of getting close to him arises. From the reaching course, it should be possible (6) to head up towards the wind and check sheets to slow down. (7) Now skilled handling under sail takes over and the man in the water should be brought under the lee side, with the yacht stopped and wind very slightly on one side.

Lifting out techniques, widely described elsewhere must then be employed. Letting go lifelines is not recommended by this writer, or more persons could be lost overboard. The physical strength of the crew has a major influence on how to cope here, as does the condition of the person in the water, which again is affected by the sea state and temperature. Expect any such occasion to be different from any training – the latter being quite rightly urged by all authorities.

Using special regulations

The ORC special regulations are reissued each January and it is well worth obtaining a set from the national authority in which ever country you are based, or from the international office in London. Already we have agreed that the fast cruiser is unlikely to be fully equipped to the rules, but they remain a *very authoritative equipment list* of international standing. There ought to be good reasons or considered alternatives before any item is abandoned.

There are preliminary paragraphs which explain to the racing man that the race organizers cannot guarantee safety at sea, but that the latter is 'the sole and inescapable responsibility of the owner'. For racing, boats may be inspected for rule compliance, but how this is done varies between different fleets and regattas. The boats to which these rules apply, IOR boats, can be as small as LOA 20 ft (6 m) or 'maxis' at 80 ft (24.5 m). There are no less than five categories of race which means different parts of the itemized rules apply, but here we will take category 2, which in effect means boats in open water. In the stricter ocean categories, there are only a few extra items which are recommended to the fast cruiser. These are a slightly smaller cockpit volume by definition (Fig 7.7), water tank divided into at least two separate containers, set of international code flags (!), and twelve rather than four parachute red rocket flares. For very long ocean races, a *watertight bulkhead* 15 per cent of the vessels length from the bow is required and an EPIRB (emergency position indicator beacon). Another long voyage requirement is the use of *jack-stays* along the deck for crew safety harnesses, but surely the fast cruiser should have these even for a short passage. Without them harnesses do not serve their purpose.

As few builders provide a *jackstay and anchorages,* you will have to fit your own and you can ensure the gear is sound. Plastic covered steel wire with eye splices is suitable and the end near the cockpit can well be shackled to a stanchion base (which itself must be through-bolted). The forward end can be shackled to a deck plate specially bolted for the purpose. By having shackles, the jackstay can be removed for inshore sailing or in harbour, where it can cause crew to slip as it rolls underfoot. It is also important to have short jackstay wires near the wheel or tiller and in the cockpit, so that crew in the cockpit and steering are held tightly on their harnesses if that part of the boat is swept by a sea.

The drill in bad weather is to pass the end of the harness out of the companionway and allow it to be

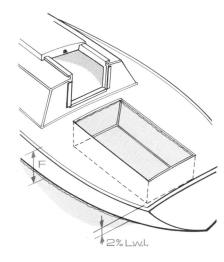

Fig 7.7 Cockpits on yachts going far offshore should be limited in volume to 6 per cent of loaded water line times maximum beam times freeboard abreast cockpit. Note definition on page 144 shows 9 per cent for ordinary seagoing.

7.5 Safety in the galley with crash bar, cook's belt, swinging stove which cannot lift off, ice box lid is hinged.

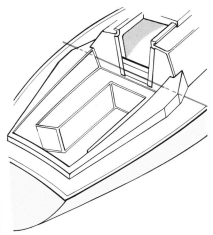

Fig 7.8 It must be possible for crew to pass through a companionway with it already blocked off to coaming level.

hooked on to these short cockpit wires by someone already there. Only then does the person below come through the hatch into the cockpit. When someone wants to leave the cockpit to go forward, he changes his lanyard from the cockpit wire to the deck wire. The deck wire would not normally be sited conveniently for hooking on from below. For extra security the harness can have two lanyards: secure one before releasing the other, or use both together for steadying purposes and exposed work in severe weather. In large yachts or those with unusual deck layouts, extra jackstays can be fitted, rather than a single deck wire.

'Special reg' features for cruising

The ORC special regulations without their preliminaries, and addenda which have just been explained are listed in an appendix starting on page 144. Among these preliminaries it states that yachts must be self righting, but this term is not defined. Equipment has to remain in position with the yacht at 180 degrees inversion and this rule should be judged to mean heavy or dangerous gear, since every saucepan cannot be held. (P 7.5). There exist lead acid batteries which can be inverted without spillage, though few yachts seem to carry them. The rules are then divided into structural features, (a broadly embracing term), lifelines, stanchions and pulpits (their own section because they are so difficult to define as an actual rule), accommodations, general equipment, navigation equipment, emergency equipment, safety equipment.

Structural features. The emphasis is on being watertight and control lines through the deck are banned.

Companionways, in other words the way into the accommodations, is well defined. Blocking arrangements must be such that if the wash boards, hatch boards or doors are below main deck level (Fig 7.8), then some part of the blocking must shut off the water while persons can get in and out. On large yachts, it is better to have the hatches well above deck level; for cockpit entry systems then a bridge deck can meet the requirement and is essential if the cockpit opens aft; if you have to have an open 'door' to the cockpit, then mobile blocking off is acceptable.

In bad weather many crews seem reluctant to close off their main hatch with all the washboards, but I have never felt this and I have been saved by this total closure. Often there are reports of heavy water entering through an open companionway. The total blocking arrangement must be capable of being locked whether the hatch is open or not. (Fig 7.9). It must be operable from both inside and out, so no one is locked in or unable to get in. Many

Fig 7.9 This top wash board lock can alternate by lever operation, to bolt to the hatch or the side. Levers are on both sides, so crew can control entry or exit. With side lock, wash boards are held with hatch open or openable. With top lock hatch is secured and this position is also used as a lock when boat is left unattended on her mooring.

production hatch arrangements do not comply with this proviso. Even this is not enough, since wash boards can be lost as they are being inserted or when only some are in. Lanyards are therefore needed to prevent loss and a lanyard threaded acts to hold them in position. Remember it is easier for washboards to fall out of a 'tapered' rather than a 'straight' companionway, but lanyards probable overcome this anyway. (Fig 7.10). Washboards should in all cases be very strong at least 3/4 in (35 mm) probably teak and the retaining channels must be proof against impact on the washboard (screwed-on flanges are a waste of time).

The formula for cockpit volume is a useful guide: modern cockpits are not often a problem in this way, but remember that lockers which can fill with water are part of the volume.

General equipment. Bilge pumps are carefully specified and they cer-

Fig 7.10 To prevent loss of washboards, a lanyard runs through eyes and is tied to the top one by tightening up on the cleat. When washboards are stowed blow, lanyard is kept threaded, so they can never be lost. For day sailing, or in harbour untie lanyard from top washboard, unthread and coil away round the cleat.

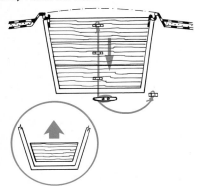

tainly deserve thoughtful installation. A basic requirement is that pumps must be operable with all hatches, seats and lockers shut. At least one must be on deck and one below. Modern diaphragm pumps are rightly the favourite in yachts and one of these can emerge through a watertight seal in the cockpit. Its handle will probably not be permanently rigged as it will foul gear, but it should be mounted close by in clips and permanently affixed by lanyard, this latter being rightly a rule. In a crisis you cannot be looking for a pump handle, yet it has been known! Even in small yachts the whole plumbing arrangement for the pump must be permanent with no question of having to place pipes over the side and so on. The pump or pumps down below can be in any convenient position. One can discharge through a heads exit pipe, so long as this has an inverted 'U' above the waterline and hefty change-over valve.

A major difficulty in all modern yachts is to get the bilge water to the inlet of the pump (complete with its strum box, of course). With the inlet amidships and the boat heeled, not necessarily a dangerous amount of water will evade the pump, but certainly enough to make conditions very unpleasant below. One answer is a *sump* mentioned earlier let into the top of the fin keel (Fig 7.2); even then sponge and bucket should be available below. Sponges permanently set under the cabin sole will also stop water running rapidly up the bilge on heeling, but they have to be wrung out from time to time.

Torches (flashlights) are a small but important item. Strangely the rule here only calls for resistance to water. Better is to have either a number of cheap torches modified

with plenty of boat tape and/or underwater type diver torches which can be thoroughly drenched with spray, rain and solid water. I have used both with success and the rule is wise to mention spare batteries and bulbs.

Emergency equipment. In this section are the important dimensions for *storm sails,* the use and design of which we have discussed but not yet the dimensions and detail. A common fault is that storm sails are too big and they do look ridiculously small when hoisted for practice (as should always be done to ensure all fittings are compatible and complete) in fine weather. For the tactics suggested in the previous chapter, small size is essential. A fast cruiser, which by way of a trial hoists these sails in a 35 knot wind, will get along amazingly fast. Try this. In this special regulation the maximum size of the *trysail* is 0.175 P X E (P being the length of the luff of the mainsail and E being its foot). It should have neither battens nor headboard and must be able to sheet independently of the main boom (in case this is broken or because it is more likely safely lashed down with the mainsail on it). Sail number will be on the trysail as identification and the whole thing in a cloth of fluorescent orange is very useful. It means the yacht can be spotted more easily and the sail is unmistakable when being pulled out from below. The trysail can go up the ordinary groove or track on the mast, but must also have eyelets so that it can be laced if necessary. It can be sheeted to both quarters and the arrangement has to be worked out on each yacht.

No less than two jibs are specified in these rules, the *storm jib* and a so-called heavy weather jib. The latter is merely a product of sail limitation rules for racing boats and the only significance for the cruiser is to remember that the headsails in the sail plan should reduce in even amounts for increasing heavy weather. By all means use the figures in the rule (10.21.3) as a check against the headsail immediately bigger than the storm jib. This again can be orange fluorescent and must have been tried out on the yacht for its sheeting arrangements and all fittings. Sometimes the sheeting appears to come forward of the existing tracks and to get a fair lead, the jib must be moved higher on the stay by means of a strop. (P 7.6). Yet in storm conditions, it is preferable for it to be as low as possible. To solve this problem special leads may need to be sited on deck, but they are rare! Remember that this sail (more than the trysail), not only has to take extreme strength of wind, but may have heavy spray and solid water thrown at it. Its strength must be beyond question.

Safety equipment. A *lifejacket* for each crew member is basic and in many countries there are government or coast guard regulations anyway. The specification of these may also have national rules. The owner should have a set of lifejackets which he keeps stowed away in good condition for handing out in an emergency. If the crew choose or the skipper is keen to wear flotation devices when sailing normally that is another matter, but the 'ship's lifejackets' should be above and beyond anything worn every day. *Harnesses* are now considered a major aid. The

7.6 Storm jib set, but on the extremity of the track which is not the best sheeting.

ORC publishes an international minimum standard for a *yacht safety harness*. In commercial terms it is a developing area and an increasingly expensive one! There are certain features which are important (Fig 7.11) and it is an item on which literally ones life can hang. A number of the recommended points for harnesses are basic, but others have sadly been the result of accidents with designs that have failed, resulting in deaths at sea. For instance the requirement that it must be impossible to clip the harness on incorrectly was the result of well publicized cases where certain belts pulled open. The thickness of the securing line is related to the loads which a man may put on it when thrown across its full length. Wrong hooks on wrong anchorages have been shown to open. Looking after harnesses is important. My own drill is to hand a harness to each of the crew before we leave harbour. He or she adjusts this to suit the outside of his foul weather clothing and then writes his name with indelible felt pen on a piece of boat tape firmly wrapped on the harness. Thus each harness is *working* and *identifiable* . One further point is not to lose it, after going off watch and turning in. Each crew person should hook his own harness on somewhere he can grab it instantly – harnesses have a habit of hiding themselves!

Life-rings are the immediate aid for a man going overboard. Under the rules one of these has to be elaborately equipped with a pole and flag as well as much else (Fig 7.12). The rule says the pole must be permanently extended, thus the sight of racing boats with the dan buoy and its pole stuck up in the air by the stern. Cruisers can use special tubes

in the transom if they have them. The difficulty with all this equipment is releasing it quickly and thought must be given as to how it is stowed. The second life-ring, only has to have a drogue and a light. It may be easier

Fig 7.11 The ORC has some minimum standards for a yacht harness. This apparently simple device has taken much development to make it a real life saver. Standards (mainly based on AS 227 and BS 4224) include recommendations on width of load bearing strap 1½ in. (38mm) and braces ¾ in. (19mm); avoidance of the buckle ever slackening; materials of straps, line, thread, fittings and hooks; sewing and splicing. Tests are available for non-magnetic properties and dynamic load by dropping a dummy.

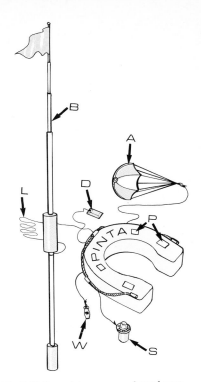

Fig 7.12 Complete man overboard gear. Thought must be given on each individual yacht to stowage for really quick release, yet with no possibility of the gear being lost or damaged in heavy weather. Equipment consists of horseshoe life ring, with whistle (W),dye marker (D) and drogue (A) with (S) self igniting high intensity water light and pole with flag (B) which will fly 6ft. (1.8m) off the water. P is fluorescent patches and L is line of 25 ft. (8 m).

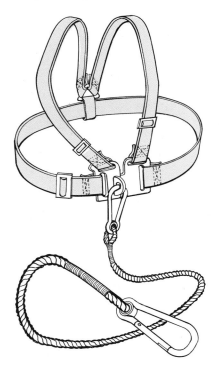

to throw the lightly equipped ring first and then have the more complicated one for a 'second run', dropping it near the man in the water. On the other hand, the idea of the pole on the buoy is to be able to spot the location as the yacht returns to the rescue. It is difficult to argue with the extent of equipment specified, so it needs working out how it can best be used at sea.

The major item among the safety equipment is the *life-raft* . (P 7.7). These have saved many lives, but there have been casualties in them as well. Their development for yachtsmen has no doubt only just begun. National and international bodies all have their own specifications, while the manufacturers struggle to keep the price down, so that people will indeed buy their rafts. Most equipment works because we use it frequently, then modifying it or maintaining it as required. In the case of the life-raft, we hope never to use it and most sailors, of course, do not. All trust has therefore to be placed in the sealed

container behaving in every respect, when it is brought into use in extreme conditions. In previous years the main problems with rafts have included (a) finding the loose equipment inside is not secured or of bad quality, so that it is washed away or fails to function, (b) the inflatable rings splitting, sometimes with the whole canopy being blown away, (c) capsize, sometimes repeatedly in heavy seas, (d) sea anchor failing to function and being difficult to handle.

As the technical points are complex and arguable and as various different authorities in different countries are involved, the best recommendation is that owners should try and follow the latest specification and also be aware what it is they have purchased. Remember there are significant differences between big ship and yachting rafts and that the stowage of a yacht raft may make it vulnerable to damp, quite unlike a raft in a solid container, high up in the structure of a ship. This is one reason why yacht life-rafts should be

given an annual service; during this it is fully inflated, maintenance carried out and equipment checked. If you are on a long voyage, the test may well be at longer than one year intervals!

A *grab bag* makes sense. Essential food and equipment are ready below decks when on passage but together in a bag. In the event of abandoning ship into the raft, the bag goes with the crew. It is interesting to make up your own bag: everyone will have his own priorities, but here are some recommendations:

Fresh water in secure small containers.

Non-thirst provoking food rations, sweets, barley sugar, seasickness tablets.

Drinking vessel graduated in 10, 20 and 50 ml.

Tin opener.

Knife and other small tools.

Illustrated table of life-saving signals.

First aid kit.

Red parachute and hand flares.

Daylight signalling mirror and signalling whistle.

Two throwable floating lamps or 'cyalume sticks'.

Reserve sea anchor and line.

Remember the life-raft already has certain equipment to scale sealed in it, in accordance with its specification. If the yacht's flares are all normally kept in a bag on board, then that bag can be grabbed and placed in the life-raft, when boarding in an emergency.

Locating important equipment

A delivery crew on a famous yacht some years ago ran into a severe gale when only about 25 miles from their safe destination. Being on a lee shore they needed the storm jib badly, but

101

it could not be found. The yacht foundered with loss of life and the lack of a storm jib was said to be contributory to this. The sail had been on board and the regular skipper, who was not on the passage, would have known where to find it. It is therefore important to have all important equipment locations listed. Even the owner can forget where he has stowed things, but for everyone else these lists can be vital. (P 7.8).

A sail list is quite common and this usually shows a list of all sails, how each bag is marked, its area in square feet (sq m), wind force in which it is used, sheet lead position and the location of the sail in normal stowage. This causes few problems, but it is all the small (and large) items which may be needed in a hurry, yet are in different parts of the boat that cause problems. There follows an example of a location list. Obviously every yacht will have different items on the list and different types of locker and stowage. The storm sails (trysail and storm jib) should be on this as well as on the sail list. The lists can be typed on waterproof paper such as 'polyart', which cannot deteriorate in damp conditions below. Boat tape will secure this to a bulkhead where all can see it.

Far forward. Boarding ladder, radar reflector.

Alongside anchor locker. Trysail, storm jib, boat hook, long warps.

Hanging locker. Bosun's chair, bolt croppers, large hack saw, mobile bilge pump, roll of seizing wire.

Starboard saloon berth. Emergency steering gear, spare water containers.

Under chart table. Grab bag,

main tool roll, snatch blocks.

Chart table drawer. Small hacksaw, large and small hacksaw blades, spare bulbs (all lights), all small fitments (split pins, small winch spares pawls), screws, bolts etc, glue, oils (release fluid etc), dry battery spares.

Toilet. First aid kit, other pills. Life raft instructions inside the door.

Locker port inside companionway. Harnesses, handy billy, backstay special tackle, bag of shackles, thimbles etc. Fog horn. Engine starting handle.

Quarter berth locker. Bag of flares (yellow bag), lifejackets (blue bag), spare winch handles, spare sail battens, engine spares, vent storm caps, spare tiller, tool roll for engine, emergency antenna, dinghy repair kit, sail repair kit, sail number on canvas screen, spare sail tyers (in red bag).

Locker aft of galley. Soft wood plugs, portable vice, spare vice, spare small line in green bag.

Galley bottom drawer. Spare dry matches in plastic box, spare tin opener.

Chart table book shelf. All instruction books and cards for equipment on board in plastic envelope, first aid manual.

An alternative system is to list everything in alphabetical order and then write the location against each item.

8. Fast navigation

In attempting to make faster than normal passages, good navigation forms an essential element. This is well demonstrated at the end of an offshore race, if you listen to the comments of competitors. Before the event they will be concentrating on the technology of their boats, sails and rigs; after the race they will (except for the winner) be explaining how they tacked too early, got set a mile one way or the other, or failed to pick up a mark! In other words the seconds per hour gained by smart sailing and equipment are often nullified by the minutes per hour lost in sailing the (slightly) wrong course. You can therefore see that 'good tactics' are required for fast cruising.

The object is to sail the shortest distance through the water and this is not always as easy as it sounds. One more example from racing is of value. A leading club was researching a new handicap system and asked all competitors during a season to submit logs after each race. It was found that the boats with the best performance had actually sailed less distance than the others over the same nominal distance course. Think about that.

For cruising, the navigator may be someone with no other job on board, or the skipper may combine the task, or perhaps the cook (not much time on deck in that case!). The fact is that except for the very shortest passages, someone has to look after the navigation. You may find yourself in charge of this department in any boat and it may be necessary to organize some of the equipment before setting off. Basic navigation is learned by many in classes or from books and I am assuming that you have these behind you. There are plenty of basics to be learned and sometimes government rules to comply with, but what is written here is based on experience of navigating sailing yachts:

something of the knack, if you like, and techniques which have proved themselves.

Nothing is intended to contradict material learnt in the class room or in official examinations, but the fact is that these cannot hope to reproduce the conditions and tensions on board. For instance the yacht may be moving quickly towards a coast in the dark, lights have not been identified, some of the electronics are 'on the blink', everyone else in the crew is busy reducing sail as the wind freshens, except for the helmsman who is shouting that he is not happy with the course and can he please have a new one to clear the shoals.

Electronic aids

Modern position fixing system have eased the whole task of navigation. Such methods are considered later in this chapter. When working fully, Loran or Decca give a continuous position and nothing else is needed.

8.1 Navigator's seat and belt with chart table bottom left. Visible also part of bookshelf, depth sounder and VHF.

However a very senior Admiral recently said that even on Polaris submarines, he recommended that the captain kept his dead reckoning up to date in the ordinary way. Whether this happens I do not know, but the remark was to yachtsmen and they are well advised to remain able to navigate by 'traditional' methods, especially keeping up their dead reckoning. This is because (a) the electricity supply may fail or the instrument or its antenna break down; (b) the navigator may be on a yacht without such devices; (c) he may be in waters not covered by the system with which the yacht is equipped (even though certain systems are world wide (satellites), at the time of writing they are not continuous); (d) a check can be kept on errors, perhaps wrong setting or

misreading. The writer appreciates that, every year, electronic navigation gets more fool proof, is less expensive, provides, more facilities and is increasingly relied on.

Equipment

Modern high performance boats really do move through the water at a speed, where the navigator may find he can hardly work out everything in the time available. So everything must be usable with ease in any conditions. Remember that in very bad weather navigation has to continue when almost everything else has stopped: hot food would be impossible, the bunks useless because the crew cannot sleep, sails have already been reduced to the smallest, helm perhaps lashed — but in all this navigation must continue and the position must be known. Even in the smallest offshore racing boats, a chart table will be found and there is a good reason for this. It is the basis of efficient navigation: a good chart table is a pleasure and also a major safety aid whether the vessel is heeled or rolling, wet or dry below. If it can be positioned or screens installed, to cut out spray, so much the better. An athwartships chart table meets these requirements best. It should have a *deep* fiddle fore and aft and preferably no fiddle athwartships, though a slot here to take the edge of the chart stops slippage and prevents chafe. (P 8.1). Size is not critical, since the chart can be folded to suit the area being used. It is all very well having a table to fit a folded standard chart, but when you fold it you may find that it is viewed sideways! Many yachts have this arrangement, with the navigator sitting on the head of a quarter berth; on large yachts, he will have his own

padded stool or chair. Essential equipment for him is a belt with the ends shackled to strong points through bolted. This is worn once the yacht is heeling with the chart position to windward. The belt can alternatively double for the cook, assuming the galley is on the opposite side. (P 7.5).

A fore-and-aft chart table can often be larger in area, but it means that the navigator is being tipped over it on one tack and trying to stop everything dropping into his lap on the other.

Plenty of vertical space around the chart table is useful. Too often one sees bulkheads just forward of the chart table cut away, so reducing area available for instruments, pencil and dividers racks, deviation and tide tables. Most chart tables have chart stowage under a lifting lid: if you are planning for a long voyage for the first time, it will be found amazing how many charts can be crammed into space, say, just 3 inches (75 mm) deep. More than one hundred charts could go in, but they must be clearly marked along the edge. Charts from different countries vary in this respect.

Each navigator has his own favourite plotting instrument, so I will only say get whatever suits your way of navigating. (P 8.2). What are a waste of time however are traditional parallel and roller rules. They have to start off on a compass rose on which variation has already been calculated and slid across the chart, or rolled, and how do you know they have not slipped on their way across (or vice versa if a bearing is being read to a compass rose)? Anyway French charts do not have compass roses! My own preference is for a solidly made protractor, which hap-

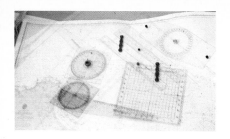

8.2 Some plotting instruments. Everyone has his favourites.

8.3 An athwartship bookshelf makes sense when the boat heels.

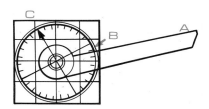

pens to be called the Hurst. It has a 360 degree compass rose which can rotate and be clamped as necessary on a square transparent plastic piece with simple vertical and horizontal grids on it. An arm swings from the centre. The grids on the square piece enable the instrument always to be positioned square wherever it is on the chart. The circular scale is clamped to read the local magnetic variation and the arm on a bearing thus reads magnetic bearing. Many other instruments work on much the same principle. A slightly different system, but equally fail-safe is a rule clamped to extending arms on the edge of the chart table; this can be moved across the chart on a given bearing, so long as the chart is clamped.

The advantage of the plotters which have the magnetic variation set in is that all plotting can be done in magnetic and no conversions are necessary from true to magnetic and vice versa. Navigation classes are fond of spending much time in working out true, magnetic and compass courses and bearings, but at sea a plotting instrument can eliminate this (Fig 8.1). Sailing yachts of wood or plastics seldom have any deviation that matters. It does become necessary to convert between true and magnetic when extracting bearings from a book of sailing directions or azimuths from an almanac

or way point bearings from a Decca or Loran set.

Among simple but important aids at the chart table, there must be a rack on which to replace pencils and dividers every time they are used: they cannot lie on the table. Have an ordinary pencil sharpener, it saves cut fingers and black charts. A long ruler is useful for various work on the chart. For books required by the navigator (almanacs, tables, tidal stream atlases, sailing directions and so on) a deep shelf outboard is usual (P 8.3). The books should either sink below chart table level or have a deep fiddle (perspex enables the titles to be read). Those little teak bars are traditional, but only work when the bookshelf is full up. A light on a flexible stem is usual and a cone over the bulb that can regulate the amount of light flooding on to the chart. A chart magnifier which illuminates or small torch (flashlight) is often needed because the fitted light is not quite in the right place. The magnifier is best secured by a piece of line. Note that fluorescent lights can interfere with radio reception and other electronics.

Basic instruments

Most fast cruisers will have more than just basic instruments. It is worth remembering what is basic and essential to navigation, because if everything else fails, these must

Fig 8.1 Some kind of instrument which 'builds in' magnetic variation prevents error and saves much time navigating. Here, the arm A reads a magnetic bearing on the compass rose B which in turn is already set at correct magnetic variation against an alignment with true north (C). Chart protractors of this type also have advantages over parallel rules and set squares in that they can be quickly and even roughly aligned on the chart for rough bearings or rough courses when making decisions about, for instance, the next tack or safe bearing of an object.

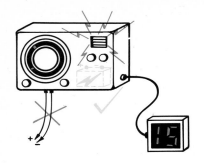

Fig 8.2 Main features of the echo sounder, one of the ultimate safety aids; it should be independent of main instrumentation. With the main unit at the chart table, reading in various units and the alarms and other devices, the repeater in the cockpit should be digital with the same unit (feet or metres) at all times.

Fig 8.3 To check the compass at sea it is possible to use a bearing of the sun rising or setting anywhere in the world. A table in almanacs gives a bearing of the sun against approximate latitude and the sun's declination for the day. The latter is obtained from standard tables. It is necessary to apply magnetic variation and due to refraction the bearing should be taken when the lower limb of the sun is a little over half a diameter above the horizon.

July 11
Latitude = 45°N
Sun's declination for day = 21°56′N
From table sun's bearing = 58.0°
This means sun rises N58°E = 058° true
                sun sets N58°W = 302° true

For instance, bearing of sun at sunset was 309 by compass. Local variation was 5°W, so deviation is 2°W on the course the yacht is steering. Check this agrees with the deviation card in use.

not. Basic are the compass, the log, or some form of distance measuring instrument and the depth sounder (or even more basic a lead line). On a very steep-to coast the latter may not be of great help, but most other places the depth sounder is a basic aid. After all if you are skirting or heading for a shore and the distance run is uncertain or the course made good doubtful (leeway or helmsman error perhaps), then the depth sounder gives an immediate 'now' reading. It tells you, for instance, that you are safely outside the 5 fathom (10 m) line or whatever it may be. For that reason I recommend a depth sounder independent of other instruments and running on its own dry batteries (or dual mains – battery). On all sizes of boat you need one reading at the chart table, which will probably be on the main instrument and a repeater in the cockpit. (Fig 8.2). The dial in the cockpit, should be of a design which reads feet only (or metres only) whatever the main instruments may show. Then in shallow water, there is instant depth given without doubt about units to those on deck who may need the news urgently.

As for the *compass*, the problems of siting the steering compass have been discussed in Chapter 3. A fast cruiser should have several compasses, perhaps a repeater system and a hand bearing and another on a direction finding set. One of the navigator's duties is to make sure that these are unaffected by objects of iron or steel. Particularly with bulkhead compasses make sure that nothing is placed out of sight below which could interfere with the magnetic field around the compass. Careful design will make sure that there are no shelves or lockers that are close to the compass that might take interfering items. (P 8.4)

Even more basic than this is the responsibility of a navigator to check the compasses frequently. This especially applies when coming aboard a strange boat or when starting a cruise in one's own boat. Simple checks can be made by lining up buoys and marks, or double checking with a hand bearing compass held high up on the centre line. Where there are two or more compasses they should all be checked against each other. There are too many tales of serious navigational errors, found later to be due to unknown compass deviation. Once out of sight of land it is hard to detect: it is worth learning how to check the compass against the bearing of the rising or setting sun using a simple table. It is only necessary to know the declination of the sun for that day and the approximate latitude. (Fig 8.3). The tables give true bearing, so conversion to compass reading must be made. Depen-

8.4 Twin bulkhead compasses are successful and frequently seen.

ding on compass mounting, the yacht may have to be steered so that some line such as the mast-forestay or a line of the structure known to be exactly athwartships is lined up with the sun at the right moment. Owing to refraction the time to take the bearing is actually when the sun appears to have its lower edge half a diameter above the horizon.

The third basic instrument, *distance measurement,* comes in many forms and may be part of an integrated electronic system. The impeller or sensor which protrudes from the hull must be carefully sited, since it will not function just anywhere. Ahead of a fin keel is a bad place, but off centre will give uneven readings on each tack. The best solution may be an impeller on each side with a gravity switch (another weak link sometimes). On a long trip some owners prefer to carry in addition, a traditional mechanical log line, which has a propeller on the end simply turning a mechanical recorder. Unlike compass and depth sounder, readings of distance are only required at the chart table. Usually it is combined with a boat speedometer (to read from the steering position), but the latter is not essential for navigation, though obviously it assists fast sailing.

The sextant

Since some very light weight and attractive sextants − many of them Japanese − are now available, it seems a piece of equipment worth carrying. Its basic purpose is to measure the altitude between a celestial body (sun, moon or a star) and the horizon, thus being able to obtain a position line at sea. Depending on the type of cruising and personal interest, sailors must decide

8.5 Celestial navigation is a major asset.

8.6 The sextant can give distance off against a light of known height.

for themselves if they wish to pursue celestial navigation. (P 8.5). Having invested in a sextant, perhaps with a view to practising taking sights or prior to a longer voyage, the following is useful to remember with a sextant. (a) Stowage may be difficult to find in a small yacht: in any vessel, it must be in its correct case, the case being in a dry very firm stowage and not close to a source of vibration (caused either by the engine or the rig); (b) It can be used to measure the angle subtended by an object (e.g. lighthouse or tower) (P 8.6) whose height is known (from sailing directions or chart). From a simple table this gives the distance off (in tidal waters make sure the sea level is known); (c) Other terrestrial angles can be measured, such as the angle subtended between three charted objects: these angles give an immediate fix without a hand bearing compass with considerable accuracy. (d) It can be used to see if another vessel is approaching or receding, or your own boat is drifting towards an object or shoreline, even though actual distance may not be known (Fig 8.4).

The point about the sextant is that it needs practice to become effective, so the more it is used the more accurate will be the results.

Fig. 8.4 The sextant is frequently useful in coastwise naviation. For instance, for distance off against an object of known height and for taking accurate angles between three known objects on shore which will give an exact fix.

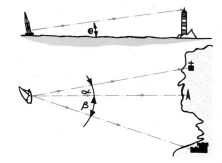

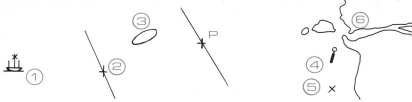

Fig 8.5 Chart markings. The recommendation is that intended tracks are not plotted and previous tracks are of no interest. Essentially what matters is where the yacht is now and the most advantageous way to get to the next mark. (Whether it is harbour entrance, turning point etc.). The result will therefore look something like this. 1 is lightship point of departure. Half an hour later an accurate fix was made at 2 using lightship and a distant radio beacon. 3 is a dead reckoning plot with some uncertainty on distance run due to faulty log. P is yacht's present position fixed by radio beacon or electronic means. The object is to reach the buoy at 4 and then make for the harbour marked 6. Estimated time to reach 4 is 2½ hours and over this period the north going current will give set of three miles. This has been plotted southward from the buoy to the small cross at 5 and course protractor is then used to read course from P to 5 and this is what is steered. Thus no lines joining fixes or any other positions are required. With the yacht now at P, positions 1, 2 and 3 are of no further interest nor are courses from them to the destination.

Preparation

If the cruise is to unfamiliar waters, it seems natural and a widespread practice to seek out someone who has been there before in order to use his experience, pilotage notes and perhaps buy his old charts off him (if he is not returning). If this is possible it obviously injects immense confidence. Without this, the voyager will no doubt procure his own charts, sailing directions and pilot books. Sometimes these can amount to quite a heavy load and it will not be possible for all the books to fit into the chart table book shelf. Stow them in sealed plastic bags to be opened when the relevant part of the cruising ground is reached. As for charts, it is always a nice decision when to buy these. If obtained too early they will not have the latest corrections, but if left too late one chart or another might be out of stock.

A list of charts on board may be tedious to make but is well worth it. When at sea and looking for a chart of an area, one then sees quite definitely from the list that the chart *is* on board and it must be possible to find it! If I missed it the first time, I must try again. No doubt the pile of charts in the locker under the chart table will start off in order, but with use, they do tend to get mixed up. The list means one is not dependent on a prearranged sequence among the charts on board.

One further tip which is arguable concerns the technique of actually using a chart. As far as possible the author tries to avoid drawing *lines* (Fig. 8.5). For instance, when plotting an initial course the protractor reads off the magnetic course with any allowance having been made for set of current or stream, deviation is

PORT DES BAINS - LANVER
Friday 23 August
High water at LA PALUT
    Fri 0700 Range 3.1
       1935
    Sat 0820   2.9
Bains H/way to La Trai 207° 7M
La Trai LH - NW Banc
      de Schole 193° 42
NW Schole - 3M off N. of
      Ile de Sept
        181° 53
N. Sept - Roscu
           6
OR N. Sept to Lanver LH 120° 25
Roscu unsuitable in   127
Ely strong wind   Miles

Stream at La Trai L.H. at
0800 1½ knots 170°(mag)
Turns at Banc de Schole
        25° 1600
Turns at N. of Ile de Sept
        190° 2230

LA TRAI LH. Fl 5s
SCHOLE E. Bn •—••— 304.3 kHz
SCHOLE E. Bn Fl (3) 20s R
SCHOLE N.W. by VQ
GRAND PIERRE LH. Iso W.R. 10s
ROSU PIER HD Occ G. 15s
      •—•—• 294.2 kHz
LANVER LN 1 Occ (2) 10 s

Fig 8.6 Even if the passage is to last several days, it is useful to have a summary of this kind for the first 48 hours.

applied in the usual way: the course to steer is then noted, but no line is shown. For bearings from terrestrial objects, the position line only needs to show near the likely position. Once the fix is made the lines can be erased. The reasons for 'no lines' are, first, to keep the chart from becoming confused. More important, second, the practice assists in preventing a 'track mentality'; that is attempting to keep the yacht returning to a line drawn between departure point and intended arrival point. At any one moment, what matters is the best way of navigating from its *present position* to the arrival point. The original track from the start point then has no relevance, not ever again. When later on, yet another fix or other position is plotted, then the new route is what matters and not the immediately previous course. The process repeats itself: the chart ends up showing plots, but not lines joining positions and destinations.

Once piece of obvious preparation is to write down basic information for the passage to avoid having to refer to books frequently. (Fig 8.6). Course and distance to each headland or point where the course alters can be shown (this answers the oft repeated request from the crew: 'How far is it to so-and-so?') Currents or changes of tidal steam can be noted. Characteristics of lights expected to be seen and buoys would be on the list and radio beacon particulars (call sign, time, frequency, range). For long voyages (more than two or three days) such a crib sheet is not so practical, but even then it is useful for the first forty-eight hours, after which routine on board will allow more time for thumbing through heavy reference books.

Every navigator will develop his own easy mode of working.

Dead reckoning navigation

As already implied, when all else fails dead reckoning navigation remains possible with the basic instruments. So the navigator keeps it going (when he has electronic and other good fixes) as a fall back position and fool-proof check. For fast cruising here are some techniques smarter than those used in basic DR work.

1. Using the kind of protractor mentioned above, *work in magnetic* and apply deviation, which in many yachts is negligible. True bearings are needed on certain instances only as mentioned above.

2. The *log book* is vital. Every book on navigation recommends a different set of columns, so I am not going to try again and experienced navigators will have their own ideas: there is a good variety on the market or you can make your own. For dead reckoning, time course and distance run are the essentials, the time being that of any course change. If there is no ordered change of course, then course steered and distance should be entered every half hour. It is best not to have times printed in the log

book, the time of the entry can be shown whatever it is. The navigator and crew may be busy elsewhere on the exact hour or half hour.

The well kept log goes with not ruling lines on the chart, for the plot need only be made up from the log when the navigator requires it. I recall one sixty-mile passage which I made without a single mark on the chart, except for a plot of the point of departure with its time and log reading. There was no option for the course, as we had to leebow the tidal steam (see below), and sail hard on the wind. As we neared the coastline of the destination, we could have tacked to reach the fairway we sought. But it was not necessary, nor was any further plotting on the chart. That is not a common occurrence, but was possible owing to the wind direction, stream and, as it happened, fine weather.

3. With a cross current or tidal steam and a variable wind, it will be necessary to *change course frequently* for best speed. (Fig 8.7). Heading towards a harbour mouth in a 10 knot wind and a cross stream, the yacht will be steering above her course to compensate. If the wind drops suddenly to 5 knots, which it can easily do, she clearly must com-

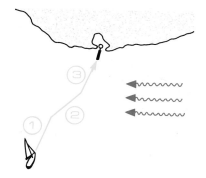

Fig 8.7 A typical course with a cross current and changing wind speed. Leg 1 will get yacht to harbour mouth to the north against west going current till the wind and therefore speed drops so she steers leg 2. When the wind picks up it changes course as seen on leg 3. In practice this can be fairly continuous if the wind fluctuates frequently.

8.7 A compass which reads above a bunk.

Fig 8.8 Back bearings are one of the most useful checks that can be made, but frequently are overlooked because psychologically the navigator and crew are 'looking forward'. Here the course is 1 and the boat is steering 1 or 1a. However back bearing 2 on the mark, that has just been rounded shows that the direction of travel is actually 2a. The navigator will then order a change of course to compensate if necessary.

pensate even more. When the wind strengthens, she tends back to the first course and so on. The navigator can calculate this, but best gives instructions to the helmsman in the form of boat speed. 'When the speedometer falls to 2½ knots, steer 280 degrees... when it is over 5 knots, steer 300.'

4. On passage the navigator should for periods watch *the course actually attained* by the helmsmen and compare it with that reported. This is one way to detect helmsman error which is one of the main variables in accurate calculation of dead reckoning position. Better still is a properly adjusted compass at the chart table or over the navigator's bunk. (P 8.7) . Some helmsmen report the 'best' course they have achieved, rather than the mean, which is a difficult figure to judge. An electronic dead reckoning calculator does the same job.

5. When sailing in tidal streams or ocean currents one has only sailing directions or tidal atlases from which to insert figures to calculate the effects of these on the dead reckoning position. All streams and currents vary with weather, time of the year and directions are not always exactly right. Every opportunity should be taken to *observe currents* on buoys, lobster pot markers and so on and compare with the directions, so that one can recalculate. Streams close in to the shore are seldom given in offical books, though yachtsman's pilots may help. After passing a buoy, tower or other mark, take backbearings at short intervals and this will show the drift. (Fig 8.8). It is an immensely valuable technique, proved on many occasions. (What is just passed tends to be forgotten so it needs a conscious effort − or an experienced navigator).

6. Do not 'look out' for marks and buoys. The good navigator will be able to *'navigate down on a mark'* from a known position. In the fast cruiser buoys will turn up where expected. It is however useful to know if one person in the crew has particularly keen eyes for distance work; I usually find out who this is and quietly make use of him or her.

Fixing the position
Methods of taking a fix are well documented in basic navigation books. A fix comes from two or more position lines taken nearly at the same time, or at intervals with the course and distance (and any allowance for leeway, drift, current and helmsman's error) known between the two sights. It is worth just checking we have the equipment to obtain these position lines. Hand-bearing compass for terrestrial objects; hand held radio direction finding antenna calibrated for any errors caused by the vessel; sextant for celestial position line, vertical angle showing distance off and angle between three terrestrial objects. Fixes from electronic aids are discussed below.

Sailing to windward
Once it is impossible to lay the chosen course because the point of destination ('the mark') is in the windward sector, then there are well defined rules for making best speed. These can be found in most basic text books, but we all forget to apply them at times. The principles are to

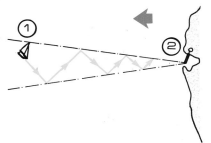

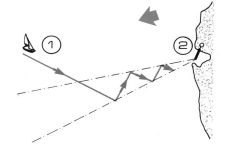

Fig 8.10 When the mark is not dead to windward, the yacht sails until it gets into the zone which is to leeward of the mark. In the same way as Fig 8.9 any wind shift becomes advantageous.

Fig 8.9 The classic system of sailing for a mark which is dead to windward in decreasing legs. This means any wind shift is generally favourable.

stay where any wind shift will be to advantage and not get caught out on a limb. Secondly, sail the tack that points best at the mark. The first principle can be adhered to by being dead to leeward of the mark; as this is not in practice possible for more than an instant, the drill is to sail up a cone of about 10 to 20 degrees (Fig 8.9). The second principle applies when the mark is not dead to windward, but in effect means that one sails on until it becomes so. (Fig 8.10).

Because we have banished the 'track mentality' there is no special difficulty in sailing a number of tacks without fixes. The procedure is the same as changing course on other points of sailing, with sailed course and logged distance noted, also along any leg at half hour intervals. The navigator must allow for leeway and wrestle with the problem of when to crack sheets in a freeing wind. Even modern boats which have little leeway are frequently to leeward of their dead reckoning position as they near the mark. (Fig 8.11). Experience shows that time and again it pays to put 'something in the bank' before checking sheets too soon after the wind frees. In other words keep sailing hard on the wind for some time after it appears that you can indeed sail a course below closehauled. Apart from weight of experience, the reasons for this include helmsman's error (straying below the compass course in a way which does not occur when steering to windward) and simply the wind failing to stay free and heading again before the mark is reached.

Cross tides and currents also complicate matters when sailing to windward. When tacking, there is often an option of sailing either with or against the current on one tack and on the other hand, across it on the other tack. The rule is to sail against a foul stream or current and across a fair stream. (Fig 8.12). If there is a steady current throughout the passage, there is no option, but when the stream is tidal and changes every six hours, then tacks should be arranged to head into the worst of the foul stream. These rules are derived from the effect of apparent wind.

A note about leebowing the stream. In Fig 8.12 you will observe

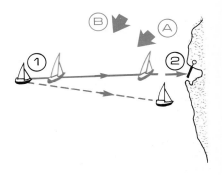

Fig 8.11 With wind direction A the boat at 1 reckons she can just lay the harbour 2. But however leeway means she ends up to starboard. In practice it would be realized that the boat was not going to lay 2 and a tack would be made. More subtle is when the wind shifts to B meaning that sheets can be freed for 2; but do not do this too soon as wind may shift back or drift or local current could mean ending to leeward. Often it is better to 'put something in the bank' keeping hard on the wind until close to the destination.

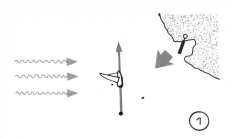

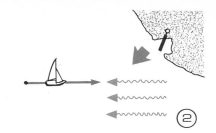

Fig 8.12 Where a tidal stream changes during a passage, then because of apparent wind changes due to the stream it pays to (1) sail across a fair stream and (2) sail against a foul stream. In this case the destination is north-east and the wind is blowing from it. The tidal stream changes at (6 hours) intervals.

that the yacht's course actually brings the stream on to the lee bow or at least dead ahead. 'Lee bowing the stream or current' is something which even experienced sailors continue to argue about the world over. The figures show the exact reason for the leebow benefit. The stream changes the true wind to give a current-induced wind which enables the yacht to sail closer: the wind also has slightly increased speed. If the stream is tidal and changes every six hours, then the yacht can be tacked at the change of stream. Subject to all the other navigational constrictions of any particular passage, she can 'lee-bow' all the way.

If the current is going to be the same all the way to the mark, with no change, then sooner or later the yacht may have to tack to put the tide on the weather bow. If the current is uniform, it does not matter when she does this (Fig. 8.13). If the current or stream is strong enough, it may be possible to fetch the mark on just one tack. Although steering 45 degrees from the mark, the lee bow tide and improved apparent wind 'push the

yacht to windward' so she makes it in one (Fig 8.14). This is a classic lee bow advantage. It does not even need much thought since the alternative tack with the stream on the weather bow is obviously useless once you are sailing along it.

The third leebow situation − and this is where the argument breaks out − is when the stream or current is very fine on the bow. Somehow it is thought that by pinching to bring the

stream on the lee bow, the boat will be pushed up to weather. All that in fact happens is that the boat loses speed, perhaps increasing leeway. The effect on apparent wind is not very different whether the stream is, say, 3 degrees of the weather bow, dead on the bow, or 3 degrees on the leebow. (Fig 8.15). Of course, it is better to have the wind 3 degrees on the leebow, for all the reasons discussed in the other cases, but there is nothing you can do to put it there because it depends on the relation between true wind and the direction of the stream. You can only sail the yacht to windward at her optimum. If this gives a lee bow stream, so much the better. As in Fig 8.13, it may after a period be necessary to tack and bring the stream on the weather bow.

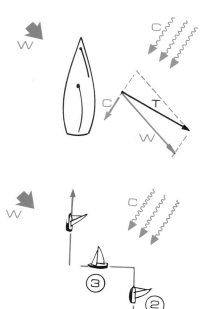

Fig 8.13 The basis of lee bowing a current. True wind W is modified by a current, C, on the lee bow. A simple vector shows that this gives a new wind (call it a tidal wind), T, which is stronger and enables the boat to point higher.

When the current or stream remains in the same direction and the mark is to windward and up-tide from point 1, then although the boat at 2 can carry stream on the lee bow, sooner or later she must tack so that the stream will be on the weather side. (3) In this case there is no special advantage in lee bowing the tide at any particular place.

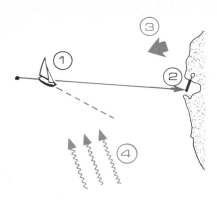

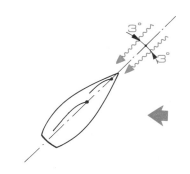

Fig 8.15 The lee bow fallacy: very small changes in the angle of the current on the bow do not make a vast difference to the resultant course. In this case there is little difference between a current 3° on the lee bow, dead ahead, or 3° on the weather bow. To prove this draw vectors for typical wind and current strengths. If such diagrams were drawn in this book, there would be no detectable difference. For best speed to windward sail the yacht in the best manner to windward: the tide will be on the lee bow if the wind allows.

Fig 8.14 Lee bowing in a 'can't lose' situation. The yacht wishes to go direct from 1 to 2 and although there is an almost dead head wind, 3, the current, 4, on the leebow and lee side enables her to do it in one leg. This is a 'true lee bow' tactic.

Off the wind navigation

Off the wind, navigation is obviously simplified with ordered courses possible to sail. Variations in chosen course are most likely to occur as a result of wanting to set running sails: these may be spinnaker, cruising chute, boomed out headsail, or other arrangement. There may also be difficulty in running dead down wind in certain sea conditions. In logging the course and distance, principles previously mentioned apply, with any change likely at the moment a particular sail is hoisted. In light weather it pays to gybe down wind for best speed, because running dead is very slow. As in beating, it is possible to get caught the wrong side of the wind shift, but in this case the penalty is having to run dead again (Fig 8.16).

As for a reach this should in theory be the easiest course for the navigator since the helmsman just steers the compass course given. Sheets are adjusted to suit the given course. However it is a point of sailing, where the helmsman can wander, yet report a fixed course, so as already recommended the navigator should observe the course steered from time to time. It is not always going to be as ordered.

Fig 8.16 Being caught the wrong side of a wind shift going down wind is not so irritating as up wind, but it is quicker not to be caught by such shifts. With the wind W1 the yacht sets off on port gybe (1), but wisely gybes over at (2) to keep upwind of destination. When she is at (3), the wind shifts to W2, so she can now gybe over and fetch her destination with the wind comfortably on the quarter (4).

If she did not gybe at 2 but went on to 5, when the wind shifts to W2 her options are either to run dead downwind at 7 or gybe over and be on an unwanted course at 6.

Electronic navigation

Micro-chip technology is now changing the way of navigating yachts in a manner never before seen. Methods previously only used by big ships can now be applied by yachts with equipment no bigger than a book of tables and electric current easily obtained from an or-

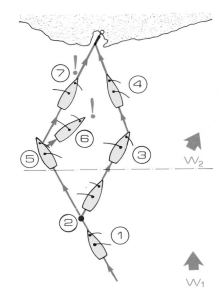

dinary 12 volt circuit. These devices are now refined, so that there is instant read-out of where the yacht is, usually in latitude and longitude, which can be plotted immediately on the chart. Sometimes this is accurate to within a few yards; sometimes the chart is less accurate than the plot.

Thus many of the old ways, as mentioned above will in future no longer be practised, but they cannot be abandoned for the following reasons. (1) The equipment, though getting relatively less expensive every year, is still a major addition to buy and install; so not all cruising yachts will have it; (2) it relies on an electric power supply and this can sometimes fail in a sailing yacht without means of recharging (e.g. engine failure) or reconnecting (e.g. wiring or component failure); (3) the equipment itself can fail or be damaged by impact, seawater or other causes. An antenna may be broken off, or the control unit go haywire and repair can seldom be made except on shore. Water may mess up an almanac, but you can still read it and a pencil can always be sharpened! Reliability of high quality yacht equipment does however tend in the '80s more and more towards 99 per cent.

There are several systems throughout the world, and sometimes in different parts of it, for instantaneous position finding. At the time of writing, (1985) no single method is most suitable for all purposes and places. This may come in 1991-92, when the global positioning system (GPS), commonly known as NAVSTAR is introduced for civilian use by the US Department of Defense. It will have eighteen satellites and provide continuous fixing coverage over most of the world. (Fig 8.17). The accuracy has

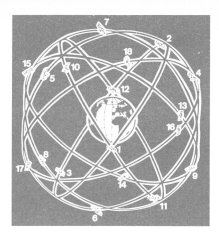

Fig 8.17 Basis of the Global Positioning System (GPS), Navstar. Eighteen satellites will ensure that at least three are available at any time to give a continuous and very accurate position anywhere in the world.

yet to be determined and it may be limited to half a cable (100 metres) for civilian use, though it will be capable of one tenth of this (for military use). So it will be suitable wherever the yacht is in the world, inshore or offshore. Alternatives to the American system may be the Russian GLONASS and the European Space Agency NAVSAT. But we have not arrived there yet.

What then is the relationship of 'ordinary navigation'? The electronic facilities wipe out much of the routine work in terrestrial and celestial position fixing. The suggested drill in coastal sailing, or passages up to about 500 miles, is to use the electronic aid and keep the log going as usual with frequent DR checks against error on the electronic read out, or other (e.g. log and compass) instruments. Radio direction finding by radion beacons (or VHF lighthouses where these exist) can be

considered a back up. The depth sounder is as important as ever. For ocean passages (e.g. more than 500 miles) the sextant (and DR) are the back up to the electronic fixing aid.

Available facilities
The table at Fig 8.18 shows what is available. Briefly SATNAV is world wide, but is not continuous and there may even be three or more hours between fixes. *Decca* and *Loran C* are continuous, but are available only in certain waters. *Omega* is world wide, but subject to weather and ionosphere interference, which the others are not. It is also less accurate at all times.

For each system there is a variety of yacht receiving sets and new ones are put on the market each year in many countries. Each will have its own slightly different method of operating obtainable from the maker's handbook. Operation, which is press-button anyway, will not concern us here. What we will do is describe points relating to the recommend system. There are then some remarks on 'waypoint navigation' and integrated systems.

Satellites (at present TRANSIT, or known as 'Satnav')
This US Navy system has operated since 1964, but only since 1980 have small low consumption receivers been available for yachts. The advantages of Satnav are as follows:- (1) World-wide fixing, 24 hours a day. (2) High fix accuracy approaching that of Decca or Loran C and considerably better than Omega. (3) Independent of weather conditions. (4) High system reliability. (5) No special tables or lattice charts required. (6) The availability of highly accurate time signals. (7)

Navigation systems

OCEAN

aid	method	basic accuracy	availability	remarks
satnav (transit)	doppler shift measurement of satellites	0.25 + 0.25 nm for every 1 knot velocity error	world-wide all weather non-continuous	average fix interval 90 mins
omega	10-14kH$_z$ hyperbolic	1 nm day 2-5 nm night	world-wide continuous	subject to interference and ionospheric disturbances
100 kH^z loran c (skywave)	hyperbolic radio aid	parts of northern 10-17 nm	central north atlantic hemisphere continuous	central North Pacific
celestial	sextant	2-5 nm	world-wide	availability restricted by weather

COASTAL

aid	method	basic accuracy	availability	remarks
decca	80-120 kH$_z$ cw hyperbolic radio aid	0-10 nm at 100 mile range	approx 240 nm from master station	coverage north scandinavia to Gibraltar & selected overseas chains
loran c (groundwave)	100 kH$_z$ pulsed hyperbolic radio aid	0-12 nm at 100 mile range	approx 1,200 nm from transmitter	coverage limited to north U.K., Mediterranean, North Pacific, North America Saudi Arabia
radio direction finding	medium frequency radio aid	A ± 2° B ± 5° C more than ± 10°	at 60 nm-2 nm at 60 nm-5 nm at 60 nm-10 nm	short range aid subject to coastal refraction night errors & interference

OCEAN AND COASTAL FROM ABOUT 1987

aid	method	basic accuracy	availability	remarks
global positioning (gps) (navstar)	satellite ranging to three or more satellites 18 satellite configuration	precision code: horizontal 0.001 nm coarse code: horizontal: 100 m 0.05 nm	worldwide, continuous, all weather unlimited number of users	

Fig 8.18 Electronic position finding systems: the options. Some coastal areas of the world have neither Decca nor Loran, so Satnav may be the best system there. Its limitations are explained in the text. It is expected that eventually the Global Positioning System (GPS) will result in a single universal method in any waters.

Once a receiver has been correctly set up, the use of the system is virtually a hands-off operation. The major disadvantages of Satnav are: (1) Fixing is not a continuous process. (2) The interval between fixes varies. (3) Dead Reckoning (DR) techniques have to be used in the interim between satellite fixes.

The system normally consists of five operational satellites in orbit, together with a ground based control organization consisting of four tracking stations, a computing centre, two injection stations and the naval observatory which monitors the satellite's time signal. The satellites are in roughly circular polar orbits at altitudes of about 1075 km. The complete satellite orbit configuration forms a birdcage, nearly fixed in space, within which the earth rotates carrying us past each satellite orbit in turn. Satellite orbit paths crisscross at the earth's axis of rotation, but are spaced apart longitudinally. (Fig 8.19). Satellites travel around the earth from north to south and back to north again at high speed and make a circuit of the earth approximately every 107 minutes. As they speed around the earth, satellites transmit on two radio frequencies-150 and 400 MHz, but only the 400 MHz frequency is used by a single channel receiver.

The comparison between received and reference frequencies produces a difference frequency. The received microprocessor is planned to count the number of cycles of different frequency in a specific time period and these are commonly called 'doppler counts'. The recorded measurements are stored temporarily in the computer memory. By comparing the doppler counts, it should receive in the yacht's assumed position from

Fig 8.19 Satnav, which has operated since 1964 but for yachts since about 1980, has five satellites. The main disadvantage is that position fixing is not continuous with sometimes three hours or more between fixes. It is therefore more useful for ocean than coastal work.

the satellite in that particular orbit; with the actual doppler counts received, the computer can resolve any differences. When differences occur, the DR position must be incorrect, so the computer re-calculates the yacht's position by progressively reducing these differences until they approach zero. After several such estimates, once the differences have become very small, the last calculated latitude and longitude is taken as the yacht's satellite fix. This is to an accuracy of half a cable when the yacht is stationary and with two cables per knot of speed when she is moving.

Errors

Generally speaking, the errors associated with Satnav are comparatively small. Many different factors can affect the overall ac-

curacy of satellite fixes. The navigator has control over some, but not all, of these factors. Remember Satnav is a dead reckoning system updated by accurate fixes. As one would expect, the fixing ability of the instrument is extremely accurate. However, fixes do occur at irregular times. It is not uncommon to obtain two fixes in a ninety minute period, then nothing for the next three hours or more. Accordingly, the DR side of the equipment is of immense importance to the navigator. Speed and heading errors in the DR can be considerably reduced by interfacing both the log and compass to the Satnav, so they need to be accurate.

The instant a fix is displayed on the Satnav, it actually refers to a time some 18 minutes earlier, approximating to the time the Satnav locked on to the satellite. Between this time, and the time it actually displays the fix, the DR 'update' that it will eventually display in conjunction with that fix, is entirely dependent on the information the navigator feeds into the Satnav. This is speed, heading, tide direction and tide speed (rate) and leeway.

Chart errors

Satnav fix computations are based on the world geodetic system (WGS 72) reference spheroid, but the nautical charts on which you plot satellite fixes are invariably based on a different datum. Usually, some correction between the two datums is required. The error is really only noticeable when using large scale charts, so when you require the highest possible accuracy and are using such charts, it is necessary to correct any displayed WGS 72 position co-ordinates before they are plotted on the chart. For practical purposes,

the error is not worth bothering about when using small scale charts. It may be one cable around Europe and up to half a mile in parts of the Pacific Ocean.

Precautions

Occasionally, users make relatively simple mistakes when setting up or using Satnav equipment. Amongst the most common errors are:

1. Setting zone time instead of Greenwich Mean Time. This always results in 'no fix' because the time is outside the required range of GMT ± 15 mins.
2. When close to the Greenwich meridian, or date line, setting westerly longitude instead of easterly, or vice versa. If the yacht's true position is more than 60 miles from the position keyed in, then no fix may be computed. The error most obviously shows up the calculation of waypoint bearings or distances, where these are relatively small.
3. With some receivers, setting the wrong 'ZONE' for the chart datum in use.
4. Failure to warm up the receiver for the manufacturers recommended period (usually at least 45 mins before a satellite rise). This is to ensure stability in the receiver references oscillator. Incorrect operation can result in 'no fix' or an inaccurate fix.
5. The use of inaccurately adjusted log and compass interfaces resulting in input errors to the receiver.
6. Leaving obsolete data in the receiver memory which immediately becomes effective again when the receiver is switched back on. Current is the main culprit, but this equally applies to heading and speed, if these are

entered manually.

7. Incorrect entry of antenna height, but this is a very small error.

8. When entering a large number of waypoints as geographical co-ordinates, always cross-check the positions entered. This is best achieved by comparing the resulting tracks and distances between waypoints by independent means or against a pre-determined passage plan. (See below).

Hyperbolic aids

Three of the position fixing systems available are known as hyperbolic navigation systems. They are: *Omega, Loran C* and *Decca,* all of which provide continuous area fixing coverage and operate in a similar manner. The general principle of hyperbolic systems is the highly accurate measurement of time delays in the arrival of radio signals from two transmitters. The distance to each transmitter can be determined from the measurement of time or phase difference and results in a peculiar shaped curved position line, called a hyperbola, whose foci are the transmitters. A major advantage of hyperbolic systems is that position lines can be accurately predicted and plotted on navigational charts in advance − called lattice charts. A disadvantage is the deterioration in accuracy caused by system geometry. Today, most hyperbolic receivers express position as latitude and longitude. Extreme care is necessary when using a hyperbolic aid. This is especially important when using receivers which express information only in terms of latitude/longitude, simply because you will not be able to make the best use of your chosen aid under difficult propagation conditions without having recourse to raw data.

Omega

Omega is the only navigational aid providing world-wide continuous fixing. The system first became available in 1968, but was only declared fully operational in 1982 after completion of the final station in Australia. For a variety of different reasons, before it had even been declared operational, the Omega system acquired a bad reputation. Today, Omega has come a long way and offers many advantages. Omega is best described as a long range, very low frequency, continuous wave, time-shared, phase comparison, hyperbolic radio aid operating in the 10-14 kHz frequency band.

Eight high powered transmitters provide global coverage. Baseline distance between transmitters are up to 5,000 miles long. They are in Norway, Liberia, Hawaii, mid-U.S.A., La Reunion, Argentina, Australia, Japan. Omega transmitters use four frequencies. The bacic frequency is 10.2 kHz and gives a wavelength of around 16 miles, which along the base line, gives a lane width of about 8 miles. Omega stations transmit on a time-shared basis and each station is identified by its pulse duration and place in the transmission sequence. At 10.2 kHz there are some 600 lanes between each pair of stations. Additional frequencies assist in resolving in which 10.2 kHz lane you are located by providing wider lanes to resolve any ambiguity. With Omega, the receiver having given a starting position, should not be switched off, as Omega is a tracking system which counts lanes from the start position. Omega receivers cannot find position of their own accord. If you only have the 10.2 kHz frequency, it is necessary for navigators to know position within ± 4 miles in order to confirm the correct lane. The use of additional frequencies greatly assists in resolving any ambiguity occuring. The 13.6 kHz provides lanes 24 miles wide; 11.33 kHz gives 72 miles and 10.05 gives 288 miles. Thus multi channel receivers offer many advantages over a basic 10.2 kHz receiver.

Two main factors affect Omega accuracy. These are out of the control of the navigator being sudden ionospheric disturbance and polar cap absorption. However Omega will remain operational until at least the year 2000 as a back-up to Satnav systems. Integrated Satnav/Omega receivers will be arriving on the yachting scene before long.

Loran C

Loran C is a long range radio aid providing reliable groundwave reception at distance up to 800-1200 miles, and skywave reception up to 2,300 from transmitters. Loran C is operated and managed by the U.S. Coast Guard. Loran C provides coverage over large portions of the seas in the Northern hemisphere, including east and west coasts of the U.S.A. and Canada, the Great Lakes and Mediterranean. Also the northern North Atlantic, around Japan and Hawaii. (Fig 8.20). No coverage is available in the Caribbean or the southern hemisphere. Two more Loran C chains are in Saudi Arabia and provide coverage over the eastern Mediterranean, Red Sea, Arabian Gulf and parts of the Indian Ocean.

A typical Loran C chain consists of from three to five transmitting stations spaced several hundred

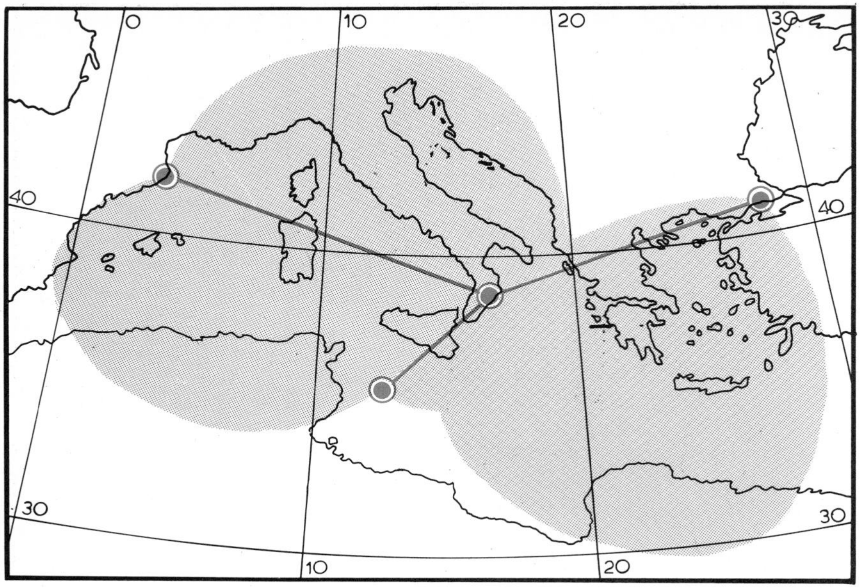

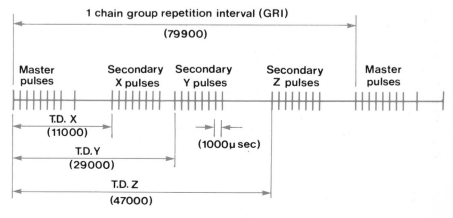

Fig 8.20 Loran C coverage in the Mediterranean. Accuracy in this area is to 0.25 miles.

miles apart and so located that signals from the master and at least two secondary stations can be received throughout the coverage area. The general principle of operation is that the master station transmits first. This signal is received both by the secondary station and the yacht receiver. On receipt of the master signal, the secondary station waits a precise amount of time − called the coding delay, and then transmits its own signal. The use of accurately timed pulse groups allows all Loran C stations to transmit on the same frequency − 100 kHz. Individual chains are identified by precise groups of pulses transmitted at a specified group repetition interval, which serves to identify the chain and prevent inter-chain interference. Chains are identified by the first four digits of the chain GRI. The same identification is used on Loran C charts and publications. (Fig 8.21).

Signals sent out from the master and secondaries are measured by the yacht receiver and the difference in arrival time, called time difference (TD) is measured to high accuracy and displayed by the receiver. The more up-market receivers can convert TD's to geographical co-ordinates.

For practical purposes, the ab-

Fig 8.21 The principle of Loran C operating from all its stations on the same frequency (100 kHz). Here the Mediterranean chain has a master GRI (see text) of 79900 microseconds. Station X, Y and Z have coding delays of 11000, 29000 and 47000 microseconds respectively.

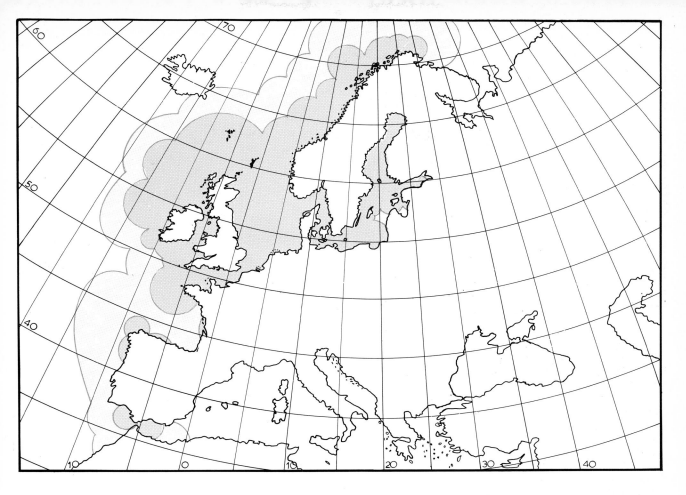

Fig 8.22 Decca coverage in western Europe is virtually complete from North Cape to Gibraltar. Loran C is only practicable north and west of the northern North Sea.

solute accuracy of Loran C varies from about one cable close to transmitters, to about three cables at the centre of coverage, and to more than one mile at groundwave coverage limits. Skywaves give greater range, but less accuracy. At ranges of about 1,500 miles position accuracy may be as poor at 10 miles, and at 2,000 miles as much as 17 miles. These are 'worst condition' values. In practice, skywave values are often much better.

Various factors can affect Loran C accuracy. Amongst these are: transmitter synchronization errors; the way in which a Loran signal is affected by land and water features during signal travel; chain geometry – gradients and crossing angles of position lines, and errors near baseline extensions. The most common source of inaccuracy is signal to noise ratio (SNR) which is best described as the difference between Loran signal strength and back-

ground noise near the Loran transmission frequency. Most Loran C sets are designed to operate with an SNR of 1:3 or stronger. SNR is of considerable importance for European operation due to the higher noise levels present. Some of the cheaper Loran sets, which are quite suitable for use in U.S. waters where there is good coverage, may not perform as well in Europe. Ensure any receiver has good tunable or automatic 'notch filters' to eliminate electronic interferences close to the Loran frequency.

Decca

Decca provides continuous fixing along the entire European coastline from northern Norway to southern Spain within about 200 miles of a master station. Decca chains are also available in India, South Africa, Australia, and the Persian Gulf. (Fig 8.22). The system is best described as a short to medium range, continuous wave, phase-comparison, hyperbolic radio aid operating in the 70-130 kHz frequency band which provides a highly accurate coastal navigation aid. The usable range is about 400 by day and 250 by night from a master station. Decca makes no use of skywaves.

A typical Decca chain consists of a master and two or three slave sta-

tions located between 60-120 miles from the master station. Slave stations are designated by colour – red, green and purple. (Fig 8.23). Decca transmitters operate in pairs: master and red; master and green and master and purple slaves. As it is impossible to measure the phase difference of simultaneous transmissions on the same frequency, each transmitter uses a different frequency which harmonically relates to a basic or fundamental frequency. Slave signals are phase-locked to a master station. Positions are therefore identified by zone, colour, lane number and fractional part of a lane. Nearly all Decca receivers in yachts only display position in geographical co-ordinates. The absence of raw Decca co-ordinates in most yacht receivers is some limitation to making the best use of the system under abnormal propagation or difficult conditions. With a set that gives raw Decca co-ordinates and with charts with special overlays, more accuracy is possible,

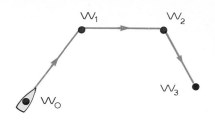

Fig 8.24 Waypoint (W) navigation has come in with electronic position fixing aids. Waypoints in terms of exact latitude and longitude are loaded into the instrument. Position can then be given in term of, say, Waypoint 2 17.3 miles bearing 92 degrees (true). Distance off track from W1 to W2 may also be displayed.

for instance at extreme range from transmitters.

For practical purposes, Decca accuracy can broadly be taken as the range from the transmitter in metres, i.e. at 50 miles, the error is about 50 metres and at 200 miles about one cable (200 metres). Decca publishes figures for both normal and abnormal conditions, and for coverage and accuracy of each chain.

Waypoints

Electronics have introduced the term 'waypoint' in yacht navigation and it will become increasingly common. (Fig 8.24). A waypoint can be either a final destination, an intermediate destination or a turning point. A waypoint is the latitude and longitude of the point of change of one track leg to the next. It can also be expressed in terms of track and distance. With most equipments, waypoint 0 is usually the present position of the yacht. Waypoints are numbered sequentially from 1. Most modern electronic equipments make

Fig 8.23 A typical Decca chain with a master and two slave situations, which are actually designated by key colours such as those. Coverage is about 240 miles from each chain. Unlike Loran different frequencies are used by each transmitter.

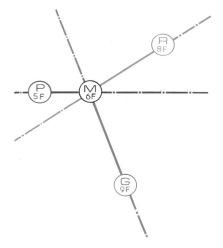

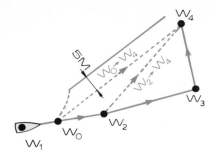

Fig 8.25 Variations in waypoint navigation. Courses and distances can be read off on the display from any present position to any waypoint e.g. WO to W4 or a parallel track held to a waypoint course.

provision for nine or more waypoints to be entered. Great care must be taken when loading large numbers of waypoint co-ordinates to prevent error. Whenever possible, it is always preferable to cross check the loaded co-ordinates against track and distance circulations obtained from a passage plan. Subsequently, at any time, you will be able to obtain the track and distance to any selected waypoint from your present position. Some equipments provide alarms for warning of the approach to waypoints or other conditions.

A navigator can initiate a change to the next required track leg at any waypoint or from the present position (waypoint 0) at any time. Alternatively, he can by-pass waypoints in one of two ways; first by initiating either a track leg change at a specified waypoint, or a track leg change from his present position. (Fig 8.25). Some equipments are likely to display cross-track error in addition to estimated time of arrival,

which show how far the yacht is left or right in nautical miles from the intended track. This will also enable a navigator to select and keep the yacht on an offset track, parallel to the current track.

Interfaces
Interfacing and compatability between various electronic equipments are subjects of importance to yachtsmen buying new equipment. Equally important is the subject of electronic noise interference between equipment. Only two pieces of wire are needed to allow one computer device to talk to another, and three if you want a two way conversation. One would think that coupling computer equipment together with serial interfaces would be relatively easy. It would be if the various equipment manufacturers adopted a common standard for their interfaces. It is suggested you make a note of the various interfaces

8.8 A well instrumented chart table. A wide range of equipment is available from all the main yachting nations.

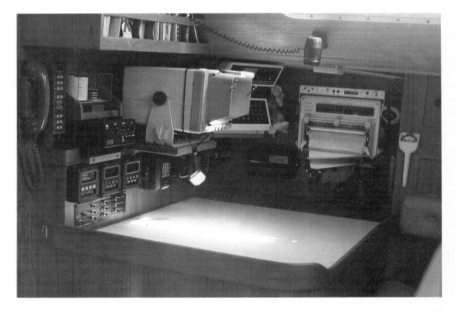

currently available, obtain a copy of the specification, and look into the problems and seek advice before buying any equipment which you wish to couple together.

If you are putting together a total integrated navigation and instrumentation system you need to ensure that interfacing standards are similar on each of the equipment bought. (P 8.8).

VDUs
Colour Visual Display (VDU) ('television screens') will assume pride of place at the navigation table and will be used to display either tabular or graphical information. The advantages of this will be considerable and will mean that navigators will obtain information quicker. Digital or analogue instruments display information numerically. Usually, such information fluctuates and it is often diffucult to obverve the overall trend. A VDU could display the same infor-

mation graphically and allow you to see the overall trend of say depth or wind information at a glance. An example of this would be in the presentation of the magnetic bearing of the true wind. For instance the series of bearings obtained from your current analogue or digital instrumentation over a given period might be follows:- 352° 349° 337° 348° 355° 003° 351° 007° A VDU could show the average bearing is 352.76°, with a standard deviation of 9.27 degrees. It could be represented graphically. (Fig 8.26). Many similar types of information could be displayed and provide more useful information than currently possible. Other options are also available. For example, a real-time display of DR or EP superimposed on a chart graticule, or even on an actual chart. Link together such information with one of the continuous fixing aids available (priority being given to the one producing the best information in your area), and a lot more useful information could be made available.

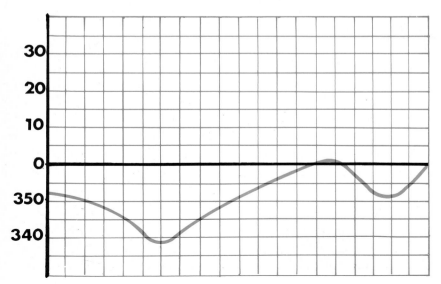

Fig 8.26 Wind fluctuation as it might be displayed on a VDU. This shows the variation of the true wind over a timed period. The computer would need to know the following to produce this: apparent wind speed, apparent wind angles to course, boat's course, boat's speed and possibly error sensors due to angle of heel.

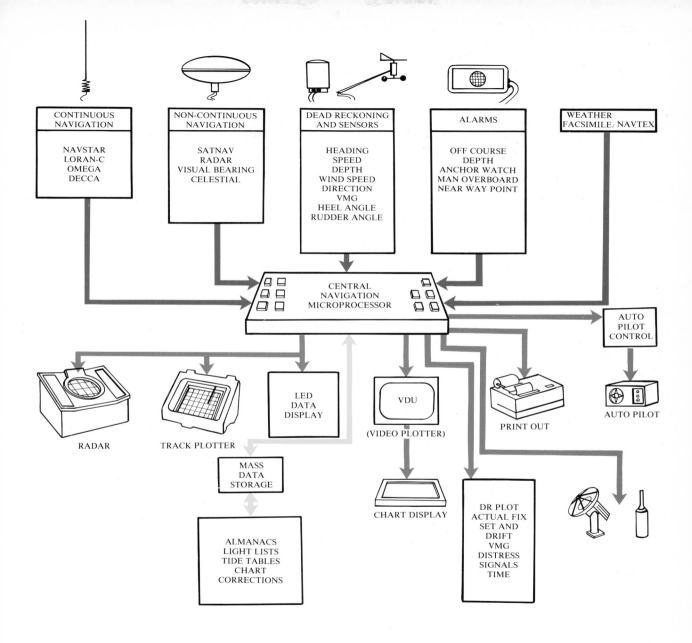

CONTINUOUS NAVIGATION

NAVSTAR
LORAN-C
OMEGA
DECCA

NON-CONTINUOUS NAVIGATION

SATNAV
RADAR
VISUAL BEARING
CELESTIAL

DEAD RECKONING AND SENSORS

HEADING
SPEED
DEPTH
WIND SPEED
DIRECTION
VMG
HEEL ANGLE
RUDDER ANGLE

ALARMS

OFF COURSE
DEPTH
ANCHOR WATCH
MAN OVERBOARD
NEAR WAY POINT

WEATHER FACSIMILE / NAVTEX

CENTRAL NAVIGATION MICROPROCESSOR

AUTO PILOT CONTROL

RADAR

TRACK PLOTTER

LED DATA DISPLAY

VDU

(VIDEO PLOTTER)

PRINT OUT

AUTO PILOT

MASS DATA STORAGE

CHART DISPLAY

DR PLOT
ACTUAL FIX
SET AND
DRIFT
VMG
DISTRESS
SIGNALS
TIME

ALMANACS
LIGHT LISTS
TIDE TABLES
CHART
CORRECTIONS

Fig 8.27 A complete integrated electronic navigational system of the future. As components get even smaller and demand less power, the use of such systems will spread. Some yachts will have parts of the system or variations of it.

123

8.9 Analogue meters on an integrated navigation system with digital read out for optional data.

Integrated Navigation Systems

An integrated navigation system is when two or more electronic navigation aids are combined together in a manner which produces a single piece of navigational data. The purpose of combining aids is to achieve a performance which is better than that of the individual system, and to provide it over the widest possible area. Currently arriving on the yachting scene are what are called 'hybrid systems' which have only two constituents, each chosen to compliment the other. Examples of this are Satnav/Decca and Satnav Loran C. The future scope of the larger integrated systems is likely to be more expansive by including radar anti-collision, autopilot and general navigational computations. Many other possibilities for inclu-sion in the central microprocessor exist. (P 8.9).

Equipment trends could develop in two ways. Single position fixing systems, either stand-alone or integrated, or all systems could be contained in one black box with its own microprocessor. A good example of the latter is the new Racal-Decca Marine Navigation System 2000 (MNS 2000) which contains Satnav, Decca, Loran C and Omega in one box. The disadvantage (other than with duplicated equipments) is a simple failure could result in the loss of all facilities. Another type of likely development for the future will be modular in concept, but designed to a common interface standard. It would be linked together as required. (Fig 8.27).

Most owners have in their minds an ideal number of crew for fast cruising. But sometimes numbers are down, yet it should still be possible to sail. By short-handed cruising is generally meant, however, a crew planned to be only one or two persons. Experience in short-handed sailing can be useful if crew fail to show or persons on board are incapacitated through illness or seasickness. If that happens the ideas in this chapter for single-handed and two-handed sailors can well apply.

Short-handed races

In the last twenty years more and more races, featuring only one or two persons on board, have been organized over longer and longer distances. Scores of lone cruisers have also made long passages without so much publicity. There is no question therefore of the feasibility and the appeal. Gear has been developed for this single (and

two-) handing, but strangely not to any great extent. On a recent tour of boats getting ready for a single-handed race across the Atlantic, the author's impression was of boats that were good fast cruisers and slightly outdated ocean racers, apart from the sponsored multihull fleet of exotics and very large sponsored single-hulled yachts.

Most gear useful to the single-hander is proving of use to the manned cruiser with the notable exception of the wind vane steering. (P 9.1). Other gear that springs to mind for the single-hander such as electric auto pilot, self-tailing winches, stowaway-in-the-mast sails, furling headsails and instant pick-up boat hooks: all these are commonplace now, for manned boats. By the way, in speaking of single-handers, two-handers should be understood as being in the same category with only one person on deck and the other frequently below. The single-

hander may want his anchor permanently on the bow for coastal cruising, a power windlass to bring in its chain and, below decks, a compass and repeat meters over his berth and alarms in his instrumentation for shallow depth, off course and wind strength rise; but this is still readily available gear.

One aspect the many races have shown is there is no single type of hull and rig that is suitable for single-handed sailing. All shapes and sizes have sailed fast and safely; indeed the special monohull, often long and narrow, has had no special advantage over fast cruising boats of the kind reviewed in Chapter 1. Water ballast forbidden in ordinary yacht racing, and therefore not widely seen, has its attractions and is a substitute for crew weight to windward, while off the wind it can be jettisoned. (Fig 9.1).

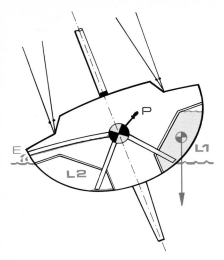

Fig 9.1 Water ballast is not often met because it is against the rules of ordinary yacht racing. It uses up accommodation space, but this is not in demand by the single hander who can use the extra weight to windward (L1). A pump (P) moves water over to opposite side (L2) before a tack. The pump also evacuates all the water (E) when the boat is off the wind.

9.1 Wind vane in action.

Techniques

As already indicated most of the single-handed techniques and gear have already been applied to ordinary cruising, fast cruising and even racing. (1) Take off sail early as the wind pipes up as the boat will actually show down if heeled more than about 25 degrees (for most modern hulls); (2) avoid the use of very 'flat' light displacement boats where crew weight to windward is essential, but even these can be converted with reballasting; (3) halyards should lead to where the sails are handled using stoppers and self-tailing winches; (4) unless rolling the mainsail into the mast (which is advisable over 40 ft (12.2 m)), slab reefing is best with all leech reef pennants ready reeved and luff pennants led aft as well, rather than cringles and hooks; (5) special rigs (e.g. Freedom and Gallant) should be considered,

9.2 Single-handed with second headsail hanked to stay ready for change.

but there is no standard solution. (P 9.2).

When alone, when and how to sleep is a major consideration. Short cat naps whenever things settle down are advisable with alarms set, both timed as well as off-course, shallow-depth etc. For a two person crew, it is useful to parcel out jobs, apart from the helm and deck work which both do. One may be cook and the other navigator. Then there may be a definite skipper for normal decisions, or whoever is on watch may make his own moves on tacking, sail changes and so on. Obviously for serious problems both persons are there to cope together. One sailor of experience tells me that if he wakes up off watch, he cannot get to sleep again until he has made sure that the other person is safely in the cockpit. Watches between the two can be at fixed regular times, or at discretion, changing, for instance when the person on watch starts to feel tired. The latter system sounds casual, but works for partners of the right temperament.

On a more grim note the watch should keep the deck log up-to-date, so that if he falls overboard, the remaining person can search in the most likely place. More than ever safety harnesses must be worn and hooked on to a practically sited jackstay; the person below is thus further reassured.

The whole question of what drill to use for self steering is one to seek advice in depth, if much short-handed sailing is contemplated. Discussion with users of boats of the same class would obviously be useful, if they have a vane. There are three requirements for self steering (1) sailing to windward, which in effect means a wind vane, (2) sailing by compass which seems to call for an auto-pilot, though the vane can be used on the assumption the wind is steady. A further variation (3) is a device to take over the steering instantly from manual without time being spent in adjustments and setting up. The latter brings us in to the area of electronic integrated systems and there are just a few in the world at the time of writing that link an auto pilot to course, speed etc on the yacht's instruments. A number of autopilots have both compass and wind vane guides, but generally by a wind vane is meant a device which requires no electricity and is purely mechanical. (P 9.3).

Points for the singlehander

Other relatively minor arrangements can make things much easier when alone or with two: once again most of these apply with slightly less force to manned boats.

1. *Instrumentation.* As well as alarms mentioned, there are now devices to switch on weather forecasts at certain times, the broadcast then being heard, (additionally through a cockpit speaker) or there are small yacht print-outs to receive forecast and navigational warnings. The more extensive and reliable electronic aids become, the less need for manpower on board. Repeat meters should be liberal. (Fig 9.2).

2. *Heavy weather sails,* such as the trisail and storm or small jib can be stowed in special positions for easy use, perhaps in a locker on deck or self draining one in the cockpit. All

connecting shackles will of course be ready rigged.

3. *Viewing* from below can be useful, when no one is on deck. A pram hood over the companionway should have a clear panel forward; an 'astrodome' somewhere in coachroof or deck enables a look around without coming on deck (Fig 9.3). It should be big, clear and with a seat below.

4. More of the *loose gear,* or some of it should be near the cockpit. For instance at least some of the white flares (for alerting other craft of your presence), one of the fire extinguishers, an immediate heaving

Fig 9.3 For looking out while remaining dry an astrodome which gives all round and aloft views.

Fig 9.2 With only one or two on board there is much to be said for repeat meters around the boat. A. Console for helmsman and cockpit with various wind readings, boat speed and depth. B. Chart table has all of A plus log, electronic position indication and major instrumentation. C. Over a bunk there is a compass heading, wind speed and alarms. D. Somewhere protected forward are wind speed and heading compass repeater useful when changing sails and working on the foredeck. E. Also in cockpit are loudspeaker, radio and remote alarms (for depth, off course, wind speed etc.)

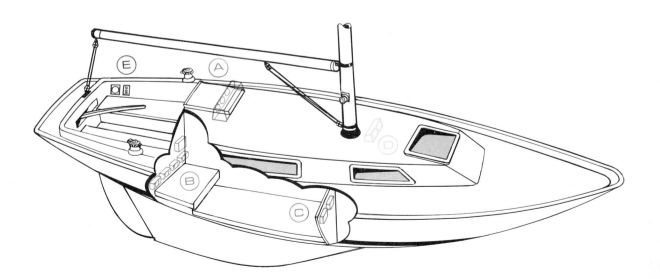

line carefully coiled, one bilge pump instantly operable without groping for handles or locker doors, binoculars mounted in a soft case, handbearing compass and stop watch (for lights): all these should be reached without leaving the cockpit.

5. *Life raft,* EPIRB and grab bag will be positioned together and be possible for one person to lift overboard. Once over, the inflated life raft will be secured by painter with a knife already in position to sever it at the right moment.

6. *Solid kicking strap* (vang) or boom *gallows* will stop the main boom falling on the crew under any circumstances (Fig 9.4).

7. *Engine controls* should be within reach of the helmsman. Engine and other tools can be laid out in pockets near the companionway, with tools less often used stowed away more securely.

8. *Fire precautions* can also include a smoke detector (because the crew may not be below for some hours) and a fuel switch off valve operated from near the helm.

9. *Food storage* can include a thermos flask with pump for immediate hot drinks and a lift out insulated food container which can be brought into the cockpit.

10. The extent of *man-overboard precautions* is a matter of judgement. Among possibilities are steps permanently suspended over the stern, a line trailing astern and a line from the wind vane, which when grabbed brings the yacht up into the wind. Though all these devices have been recommended and used by single-handers, there is no record of whether they have in practice saved anyone.

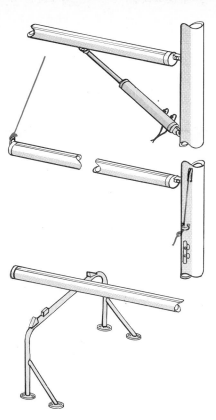

Fig 9.4 Several devices make sure that the main boom can never drop down unexpectedly. Among devices are a solid kicking strap (vang), an old fashioned boom gallows, but in modern light alloy and a conventional topping lift to the end of the boom, but with a stopper knot to prevent it falling below a certain height. In order to bring the boom right down a snap shackle is released at boom end.

10. Organized below

The fact is that the comforts of life below decks do nothing to make the yacht go any quicker through the water. Cabin furniture adds weight without strength to the boat: it can also raise the centre of gravity, so making the vessel less stiff beating to windward. As a result highly competitive ocean racers are 'stripped out' below. They have the bare essentials as required by their rules and lightweight facilities for the crew to rest, feed and navigate. The head is probably open in the fo'c'sle with no screens or doors.

Such arrangements are not for the cruising man, who will take pleasure in living below both in harbour and when on passage. When coming below off watch one prefers pleasant surroundings, some privacy perhaps; the yacht may even be his only home — at least his holiday home. For fast cruising the requirement is for accommodation that functions at sea and remains a pleasure to use

in port. While cabin arrangements can be altered without affecting the sailing qualities of the yacht, it is better to choose right in the first place, whether custom or production boat. One limitation on the arrangement may be structural features such as chain plates passing through the deck at a certain point, or bulkheads. These have to form natural breaks in the accommodation. (P 10.1). *Basic layout* in a cruising yacht and *attention to detail* are equally important. A clever plan must be supported with the functional detail that makes life below, sometimes a pleasure and (depending on the weather) sometimes at least tolerable at sea.

Layouts

Looking at the layout first, there are no end of alternatives and no end of yachtsmen with ideas as to what will suit them. The examples here can be no more than ideas for fast cruising,

with perhaps some advantages and disadvantages pointed out. (Fig 10.1). Subject to the qualifications in the comments on each of the layouts, these are ideas suitable for fast cruising. Less suitable and not shown here are numerous new yachts designed for boat show appeal, marina living and what is thought to be suitable for the charter business. The features which betray these

10.1 Bulkhead with chain plate divides accommodation.

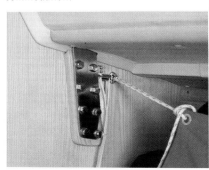

131

boats are a lack of seagoing berths; sometimes there is only one, perhaps even no berth at all suitable for off-watch use at sea. Unbelievably there are no fiddles on the edge of horizontal surfaces, maybe just a low smooth capping, as seen in a car or caravan. There may well be panelling and lining, which is not only heavy, but prevents access to the hull, or to wiring and plumbing.

With the basic layout designed, accepted or rearranged, the other half of the equation is the detail of such features as bunks, galley, plumbing and electrics. Experienced sailors know that the failure of designed arrangements and equipment can take many hours of frustration to put right at sea or in harbour.

Bunks

Double berths are seen on more and more boats, but are essentially for harbour use. I once made a long voyage sleeping on part of a dinette when off watch. On one tack I was held in place by the folded cabin table and on the other tack I was against a lee cloth; the second person on the bunk was held against the leecloth and settee back rest (Fig 10.2) respectively on the corresponding tacks. It is not a good system.

One person can presumably make use of a double berth at sea, but a narrow berth is best if she is rolling. Over the years I have trained myself to sleep soundly on my back and not roll on to my side; thus I can remain stable when the motion is fairly violent at sea. If there is a shortage of seagoing single berths, then steps will have to be taken to divide a double berth with a lee board. Then the mattress will also have to be divided; this may mean a second set of mattresses, so the widely touted double berths have their limitation in a layout.

Fo'c'sle berths are frequently double, or the feet meet forward, or a bunk piece can be inserted to give singles or double. (P 10.2). It makes sense to have a double here, since the fo'c'sle cannot be used at sea for sleeping anyway. If there is much joinery well forward, it has an adverse effect on performance. So for practical purposes in yachts other than those over about 45 ft (13.7 m) berths for seagoing are quarter berths, pilot berths or settee (saloon) berths.

Settee berths are the easiest to use, being merely a conversion of any seating space over 6.1 ft (1.87 m). All they normally need is fitting with a leecloth. They are not so convenient

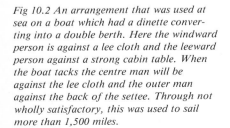

Fig 10.2 An arrangement that was used at sea on a boat which had a dinette converting into a double berth. Here the windward person is against a lee cloth and the leeward person against a strong cabin table. When the boat tacks the centre man will be against the lee cloth and the outer man against the back of the settee. Through not wholly satisfactory, this was used to sail more than 1,500 miles.

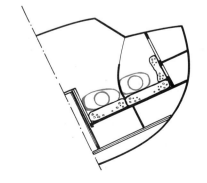

Fig 10.1 Six internal boat layouts for fast cruising; and some features for other kinds of cruising.

(1) Though this layout can be cruised, it is really an example of a production racer of 34 ft (10.3 m) LOA. It is simply four berths, a chart table under the bridge deck with a galley up by the mast. There would not be bunks for all the racing crew of 6 or 7 and it seems that day racing is perhaps in the designer's mind. The yacht is perfectly able to race long distances, because of her structure, design and rig, but going below would be miserable. Not even for the very fast cruiser! (At 6910 lb (3150 kg) she is very light. (Db2 - Germany)

(2) Almost the same size (LOA 33 ft, 10m), but more fully furnished on a displacement of 7800 lb (3545 kg). The weight has been pushed out to the ends, which is bad for speed but good for making use of cruising space. This is also a racing boat, a one-design offshore racer, but its class allows cruising facilities; as result the class has proved popular. The arrangement is a common one in yachts between 32 and 38 ft (9.75 and 11.6 m). The saloon with its table makes for civilization in port, but there are always two berths to windward if required. The fo'c'sle can be used for bunks in harbour (total seven on board) and for sails or kept fairly empty at sea. The chart table area is first class. (Sigma 33 OOD - Britain)

(3) Because (2) is such a common and succesful layout, here it is again in a slight variation and slightly larger yacht. Like both the previous boats, this is a fast light yacht (9195 lb, 4180 kg), though 32 per cent heavier than (1). It needs to be for this accommodation. There are subtle differences to (2) in the way the berths are arranged. In fact there is a shortage of seagoing berths unless the double berths in the saloon and quarter have divide boards and cloths to make them suitable when the yacht is going to windward. (See Fig 10.2). (Mull one-off USA)

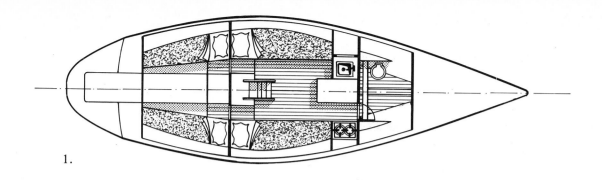

1.

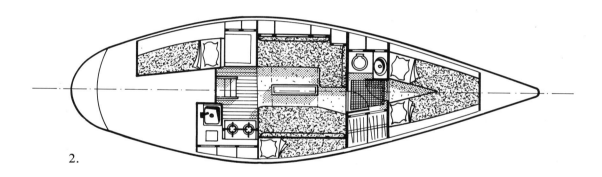

2.

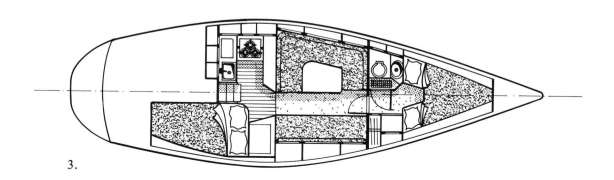

3.

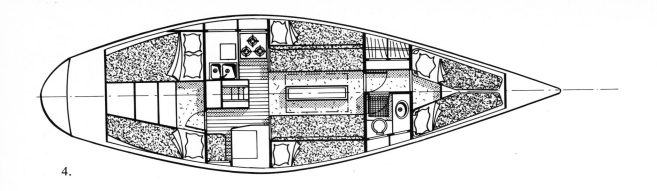

4.

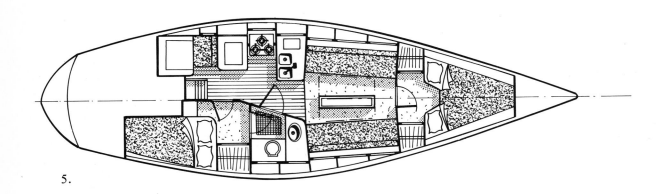

5.

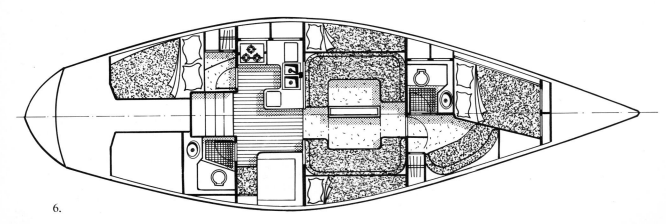

6.

(4) This is a very well appointed fast cruiser of international reputation. The extra few feet enable the designer to fit a layout that is hard to fault for fast cruising. Note the steps are in almost the widest part of the boat. One secret is that the main hatch is well forward of a big cockpit and bridge deck. Thus it is possible to have a real after cabin with a double berth, single berth, dresser, sets and lockers. The galley, navigational area and head are all where most people would want them. There are two seagoing berths to windward in the saloon, alternatively two persons can sleep in the pilot berths, leaving the saloon and its settees clear. Pipe cots in the fo'c'sle take two extra in harbour; making a scratch cabin. *(Swan 371 - Finland) LOA 36.8 ft, 11.23, displacement 15400 lb, 7000 kg.*

(5) In larger yachts the variations become wider and this one may not suit everyone, but it is the product of an experienced and original designer. The yacht is a pure cruiser: unlike layouts *(1)* to *(4)*, it has no racing pretensions, but the rig and hull are efficient. Unlike *(4)* the main companion way opens straight into the cockpit. Not even the mainsheet is in the way, as the track for it is forward of the main hatch. So the designer has put the athwartships chart table well aft, facing aft. Then the galley, unusually, comes on the same side of the yacht. The head, shower and spacious washplace is opposite. So the main saloon is pushed well forward, indeed the mast is in the centre of it, the cabin table being around the mast. Seagoing berths? Well, she is clearly not intended for a big crew, while the small crew (4 maximum ?) will have plenty of locker space. With much teak joinery, the displacement is designed at 17800 lb (8100 kg) and LOA is 18.3 ft (11.7 m). *(Golden Wave 38 - Hong Kong, Pedrick USA design)*

(6) When the length is 43.5 ft (13. m), all sorts of arrangements and separate cabins become possible and the main saloon settees need not be used for sleeping. This is a standard production yacht, the larger end of a big range offered by a manufacturer. Two double berths seems to be the basis of the layout and each has its own toilet and head. Both galley and chart table are obviously spacious and are in a sensible part of the boat. At sea the saloon can be used for those off watch. An alternative layout for the same boat had all bulkheads in the same position, but two double berths with their own cabins aft and twin pilot berths in the forward cabin (hands on a charter boat?). This is a high performance fast cruiser and although the accommodation is substantial, it is not unduly heavy, especially if constructed of suitable materials. Displacement is 18700 lb (8500 kg). If the boat was for out and out racing, there would be a saving of hundreds of pounds of weight in the accommodation. *(Beneteau First 42 - France, Frers, Argentina design)*

10.3 Settee berths, but there is nowhere to sit once they are in use for sleeping.

for other members of the crew when they want to sit down in the saloon or eat or change at sea (P 10.3). They are easy and quick to get in or out of and so safer in bad weather.

Quarter berths one supposes are often there in small yachts because there is not much else that can be fitted up under the sides of the cockpit. Racing boats often have pipe cot quarter berths, which keep weight away from the end of the boat and the crew off watch trimmed as they would be if in the cockpit: it is a good arrangement in that it keeps off-watch crew undisturbed by others and up to windward, where it is more pleasant to sleep than down to leeward. As mentioned earlier in this book, deep cockpit lockers are potentially unseaworthy and quarter berths under a watertight structure are preferable. (P 10.4). If there is a single built-in berth on each side, it can also be used for stowage of gear, if all the berths in the yacht are not required. The head of a built-in quarter berth is frequently used as the seat for the chart table: this is the classic navigator's berth in a small yacht. As navigator I have been woken at times in order to check out something on the chart table and have been able to do so without get-

10.2 Fo'c'sle berths.

10.4 A simple mattress quarter berth under the starboard cockpit seat.

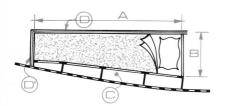

Fig 10.3 Some features for a quarter berth. Dimension A should be 6ft. 3ins. (1.95m.). B should be up to 2ft. (609mm), in order to get into the berth from forward. C is a long deep box with the inner edge as a berth board and the outer edge against a ship side and is very practical stowage. D represents engine casing or other for and aft member which forms one side of the berth. D' is low bulkhead to keep bedding from slipping off the end. Quarter berths are possibly the most secure of all once in, but are sometimes difficult to get in and out of and also can lack ventilation.

ting out of my sleeping bag! A locker down the side of a quarter berth makes excellent stowage. (Fig 10.3).

Once in the *pilot berth* , no one will worry you and if you are up to windward, it is weight in the right place. For cruising the leeward pilot berth is just as snug, but some people find it unpleasant to be below water level when heavily heeled. Assuming the pilot berth is above and outboard of the saloon settee (and optional berth), its disadvantage is possible injury when climbing in and out in rough weather and the necessity to climb over someone already in a settee berth. In a small yacht the mattress may be too close to the underside of the sidedeck, so causing discomfort and a possible banged head! If the berth is so shallow that a solid bunk board cannot be fitted, there is a moment of unease before the lee cloth is roped up. (Fig 10.4). Insulation or lining that will stop condensation is useful over all berths. Drops of water on to bedding – or worse, in the eye, are infuriating!

Plumbing

A high proportion of repairs and maintenance on board is not spent on the sailing elements such as sails, spars and ropework, but on plumbing and electrics. In the case of plumbing, water pumps fail, pipes block, leaks occur. Design of the plumbing systems on board should therefore be detailed and materials be of the best. *Sinks* are best as near the centreline as possible for good draining and should be rectangular and deep. The drain should be wide and in the case of the galley sink(s) should go to a sea cock used for nothing else. Greasy hot liquid which travels down the drain can quickly solidify as it hits the waterline level within the drain. So when laid up pour very hot water down this drain; this saves having to dismantle it afloat with the seacock shut off. Bad language will ensue if the sink is filled with water and then the drain plug pops out owing to 'blow back.' The air trapped in the pipe below the plug pushes it up as the yacht 'bobs' slightly pushing

Fig 10.4 Pilot berths are best of all according to some, especially if sleeping up to windward. In this ideal design, features include (A) length 6ft. 3ins. (1.95m). (B) head widths 1ft. 10ins. (55mm). (C) mattress 2½ in. thick (60mm). (D) bunk board. (E) access depth. (F) bunk light. (G) hand hold to get in and out. (H) netting for personal effects and/or (J) cave locker over feet.

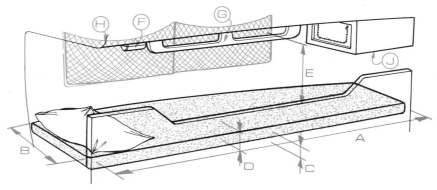

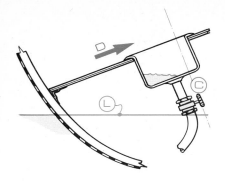

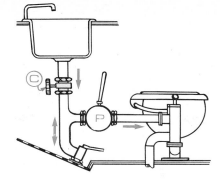

Fig 10.7 A wish basin in the head can drain into the lavatory inlet cock below basin. (C) shuts off the basin so that pump (P) fills the head by whatever system is used. When this pump is not being used water from basin merely drains out through the lavatory water inlet.

Fig 10.5 Basic plumbing for a yacht sink. Site the sink towards the centre line (D) of the yacht as far as possible to take it away from the heeled water line (L) where it could flood. Accessible cock (C) prevents blow back or flooding, but there must be a proper seacock at the skin fitting.

up the waterline level in the drain (Fig 10.5). To prevent this shut the seacock or arrange a more easily accessible cock. However the best arrangement is a pump to extract the contents of the sink. (Fig 10.6). This exit hose can have a two way cock in it, so that the pump can be used as an additional bilge pump. Not only does the pump prevent the irritating blow back, but more basically it

prevents the ingress of water when heeled, into the sink. In very bad weather shut the seacock anyway and in the first instance, if necessary, use the main bilge pump whose exit will be above waterline. Minor sinks, such as the small basin in the head which is not in such constant use need not have the elaboration of a pump, but the sea cock must be accessible. There is no objection to the sink outlet being combined with the same drain as the lavatory inlet (Fig 10.7).

Fresh water will emerge through pumps at the sink and elsewhere and such pumps can simply be connected on to the same pipe, with T-junc-

tions. If a fresh water line crosses the boat, water could leak out through the pump when the yacht is heeled if the water tank is above the pump level (Fig 10.8); a small cock in the line is the answer. As for the tanks, for fast cruising they need to be as low and as central as possible: in most boats there are few options. Strangely tanks do sometimes turn up in the cockpit area or fo'c'sle, but the weight of the water is bad for sailing ability and can even stress the hull, with such heavy weight at the ends. For short passages, keep the water supply down; there is no need to fill all the tanks just because the yacht has them. For a long voyage in

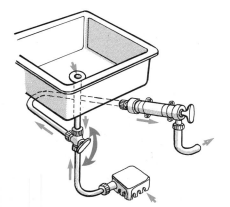

Fig 10.6 More refined plumbing arrangement for the galley sink as water being evacuated only by pump. Changeover switch enables the same pump also to be used for the bilge as an additional bilge pump (left).

Fig 10.8 Where a line for fresh water comes from a water tank (T) on one side of the yacht to a basin or outlet (F) on the other side of the yacht, then a cock (C) must be inserted in the line, probably near the fresh water pump (F) to prevent flooding when the boat is heeled with the tank above the level of the pump (right).

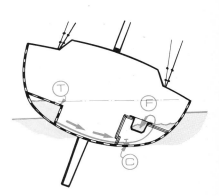

order to increase tankage consider flexible tanks. They are made of specific man made materials to prevent stagnation and remain strong. Such tanks must be lashed down for safety reasons and do not require vents as the tank 'shrinks' as the water is extracted. Non-toxic vinyl hose is satisfactory for lines, but eventually tends to become discoloured and tastes. For all tanks and lines, use a suitable water purifying tablet.

Glass fibre tanks are acceptable but are better not incorporated as part of the hull (the hull as an outer wall) because of stress and difficulty in the event of hull repair. Steel tanks are common. Tanks of marine ply and glassed edges and corners can work well. All rigid tanks need the following design features (Fig 10.9): baffles, inspection ports, draw pipe (takes water out), filler pipe, drain pipe and vent. Without a vent (except on flexible tanks), the pumps cannot function. The vent line will have to be brought up as high in the boat as possible so no leakage occurs

10.5 This deck filler opens with a winch handle.

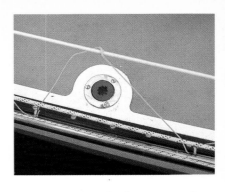

when heavily heeled. One possible place for the line to end is over the sink in case of leakage. Leading outside, for instance into the cockpit, will only eventually result in seawater contamination. As for the filler, a deck filler is usual and the latest ones are opened with the spigot of a standard winch handle (no lost keys) (P 10.5): Some people may prefer to avoid the risk of pollution through deck fillers, put up with some overspill of water in the cabin and fill direct through the tank inspection port(s). Multiple tanks can be linked by pipes with cocks. Fresh

water pumps whether manual or electric must be easy to remove from furniture and of a type (widely available now) that strips down easily. The spares locker will contain parts for the pumps.

Galley
Many aspects of the galley have already been discussed including the sink, pumps and the necessity for the stove to swing freely to a large angle in each direction and have its pivots secured totally. For the fast cruiser, even the *ice-box* can be efficient! Its lid must be hinged or secured so it

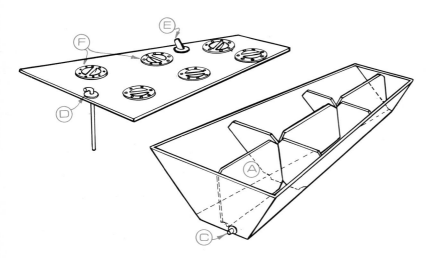

Fig 10.9 Main features of a yacht water tank whether built in metal, plywood or glass fibre. (A) is baffles further apart than 20ins. (550mm.) (B) with notches at corners, centre and elsewhere for water to find its own level; (C) is tank drain for when cleaning out; (D) is vent and (E) is filler pipe. Inspection plates (F) are essential.

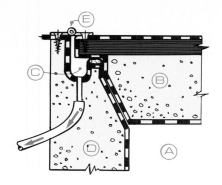

Fig 10.10 Even an ice box must be carefully designed. In this section near the top, (A) represents contents and at the bottom there must be a drain for melted ice. (B) heavy deep insulated lid. (C) drain for surface water on working top, so that messy and unwanted liquid does not filter into (A). (D) side and bottom insulation. (E) hinge or other means to secure top if yacht is knocked down.

cannot break loose, its rim must have a drain so that liquids on the galley top do not drain into it and its own drain at the lowest point to allow melted ice water to escape. (Fig 10.10). Naturally *stowage* for plates, cups and other utensils must exactly fit and wood pins can be used, if the original fiddles do not match. (P 10.6). Where curved ('soup') plates are stowed behind a high fiddle, it will be found that if piled up they will slide over one another and out: the answer is to turn them all upside down.

By the time the requirements of stove, sink and ice box have been met, there may be limited area for a *working top surface* in a small yacht. In a large boat such an area is essential for food preparation for more people. In any yacht such a surface must be surrounded by *fiddles* with a height of about 1 ¼ in (32 mm). Such fiddles are essential as they are on the saloon table and the tops of other cabin furniture. However where the top is not 'worked on' then even deeper fiddles make sense. Fiddles are best vertical on both sides but if one side has to slope then it must not be the inner side which supports the plate, mug etc. There should not be gaps in the corners, which allow knives and forks to slide out like missiles (Fig 10.11). Such gaps are sometimes left for cleaning purposes, but are incorrect. Many production boats are seen with wrongly designed fiddles and it is well worth correcting them − or avoiding the boat!

Lockers with sliding doors in the galley and elsewhere must have deep fiddles *inside* them. These are easily fitted of wood or perspex (Fig 10.12). This applies equally to doors with vertical hinges, but some builders think sliding doors are enough to prevent contents spilling from windward. Locker doors which open with hinges in the bottom edge can be opened slowly or partly to inspect contents, but even here a fiddle, though perhaps of netting is required.

Hand and foot holds
As on deck, hand and foot holds should be plentiful and very strong. Among effective *hand holds* are grab

10.6 Effective plate stowage, note high fiddles and semi-deep locker. Perspex fronts help to find items.

Fig 10.11 *Fiddles should pass right round a working top and not be left open as seen on many production boats. Otherwise the very item that you wish to retain, as this fork, are lost!*

rails running the entire length of the deckhead in the saloon, loops in half bulkheads, pillars which may also be structural, handles inside the companion way for when mounting the steps up, handles for hauling in and out of berths, extra handles in the head (too often bare in there) and any part of the furniture that is not intended for holding, but might be grabbed in an emergency, must be strong enough to withstand this ill treatment.

Small locker doors close to the sole should be avoided or someone will step on them when the boat is heeled. Consideration must be given to the surface of the cabin sole. Glossy varnish is obviously wrong, but non-slip varnish, bare teak and man-made coating surfaces are among the choices.

Electric equipment

The electric equipment and circuits on a fast cruiser will be no different to that on any other type of yacht. Because she is sailed hard it must be beyond reproach and there are no special difficulties with well installed modern equipment with a marine switch board and fuze box and circuit wiring led high up in the boat. Because a sailing yacht has no engine running, more dependence than usual relies on the batteries. These should be high capacity (ampere-hours). Check the ampere-hours recommended to start the motor and then double it. This means one (or one set of) batterie(s) can be reserved for starting the engine while the duplicate set runs all the ship's appliances (lights of all sorts, instrumentation, electric pumps, water pressure and all other navigational and domestic devices). It is worth giving plenty of attention to

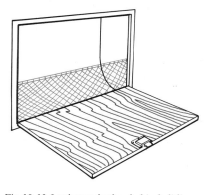

Fig 10.12 *Lockers whether behind sliding or hinged doors must all have deep fiddles to retain contents. A sliding door should have a notch at the end otherwise the movement of the yacht tends to allow the door to work its way open at sea. It is useful to hinge small lockers along their bottom edge as it is then possible to open the locker to 'peer in', but as usual a fiddle, or netting as shown here, must be in position.*

lead acid batteries and this will pay dividends. (Fig 10.13).

The switching arrangement that determines which battery is giving the power and which is isolated should be unmistakably marked. The switch also enables all batteries to be isolated (when the boat is left) or all batteries to deliver voltage.

This enables power to be reserved and prevents the batteries being charged together, which is incorrect if they are at different initial states of charge. A hydrometer should be on board as this is the sure instrument for checking the state of charge of each cell. Voltmeters will not state how much charge is left in the battery. In hot climates the hydrometer should be fitted with a thermometer, as a high temperature will give a false reading showing the charge to be lower than it really is. The plates in the battery should be kept covered with liquid (topped up with distilled water), but a hydrometer reading should not be relied on just after water has been added. Battery terminals should be coated with petroleum jelly (not ordinary grease) and the batteries be sited in containers, glass fibre is suitable, so dribbling and minor spillage does not go on to any part of the boat. Of course they must be clamped down, as mentioned earlier. A low down central position is suitable because of their weight, but not so low that bilge water can reach them easily. Ventilation should be provided because of hydrogen given off when charging, but this is not serious except at a high rate of charge, which is not an advisable procedure for long battery life.

When the yacht is laid up the batteries should be brought ashore, stored in a cool place, charged every couple of months even though not in use, not be stored on concrete or similar 'cold' surface (wood boards are better). With all this care afloat and ashore, the batteries which are the basis of the yacht's electric system will be very reliable and last for much longer than their guaranteed life.

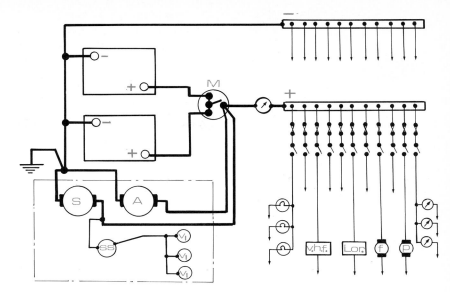

Fig 10.13 Important point in an installation of two 12 volt lead acid batteries. The engine alternator charges either or both batteries by means of careful control of master switch (M): same switch determines which battery is in use. In a sailing yacht, one battery must be left with reserve voltage to start engine to recharge. S, engine starter, SS starter switch. Positive and negative bus bars are used to take off various appliances, V. (Negative connections not shown for clarity). V1 is engine indicator lights such as amps, oil pressure, temperature. Negative line is earth, and connects to sacrificial anode and to engine casting.

Appendix

Special regulations agreed internationally by the Offshore Racing Council

This is a remarkable and precise guide for making a fast cruising yacht fit for all weather. (This is for category 2 events. These are in the open sea, perhaps several hundred miles or more, though not trans-ocean)

Commentary on these rules is on pages 97 to 101.

6.0 Structural features

6.1 *The hull, including deck, coach roof and all other parts, shall* form an integral, essentially watertight, unit and any openings in it shall be capable of being immediately secured to maintain this integrity (see 5.1). For example, running rigging or control lines shall not compromise this watertight unit. Centerboard and daggerboard trunks shall not open into the interior of the hull.

6.12 *Hatches.* No hatches forward of the BMAX (maximum beam) station shall open inwards excepting ports having an area of less than 110 sq. in. (710 cm²). Hatches shall be so arranged as to be above the water when the hull is heeled 90°. All hatches shall be permanently fitted so that they can be closed immediately and will remain firmly shut in a 180° capsize. The main companionway hatch shall be fitted with a strong securing arrangement which shall be operable from above and below.

6.13 *Companionways.* All blocking arrangements means to prevent their being lost overboard.

6.14 *Cockpit companionways,* if extended below main deck level, must be capable of being blocked off to the level of the main deck at the sheer line abreast the opening. When such blocking arrangements are in place this companionway (or hatch) shall continue to give access to the interior of the hull.

6.21 *Cockpits* shall be structurally strong, self draining and permanently incorporated as an integral part of the hull. They must be essentially watertight, that is, all openings to the hull must be capable of being strongly and rigidly secured. Any bow, lateral, central or stern well will be considered as a cockpit for the purposes of 6.21, 6.22, 6.23 and 6.31.

6.22 *Cockpits opening aft to the sea.* The lower edge of the companionway shall not be below main deck level as measured above. The openings shall not be less than 50% of max. cockpit depth multiplied by max. cockpit width. The requirement in 6.31 that cockpits must drain at all angles of heel, applies.

6.23 *Cockpit volume*

6.23.2 The maximum volume of all cockpits below lowest coamings shall not exceed 9% L times B times FA (9% loaded water line times maximum beam times freeboard abreast the cockpit). The cockpit sole must at least 2% L above LWL (2% length overall above loaded water line).

6.31 *Cockpit drains*

6.31.1 *For yachts 21 feet R (28 feet/8.53 m length overall) and over.* Cockpit drains adequate to drain cockpits quickly but with a combined area (after allowance for screens, if attached) of not less than the equivalent of four ¾ in. (2 cm) diameter drains. Yachts built before 1-1-72 must have drains with a combined area (after allowance for screens, if attached) of not less than the equivalent of two 1 in. (2.5 cm) drains. Cockpits shall drain at all angles of heel.

6.31.2 *For yachts under 21 feet R (28 feet/8.52m length overall).* Cockpit drains adequate to drain cockpits quickly but not less in equivalent of two 1 in. (2.5 cm) diameter drains. Cockpits shall drain at all angles of heel.

6.4 *Storm covering* for all windows more than two square feet in area.

6.51 *Sea cocks or valves* on all through-hull openings below LWL, except integral deck scuppers, shaft log, speed indicators, depth finders and the like, however a means of closing such openings, when necessary to do so, shall be provided.

(washboards, hatch-boards etc) shall be capable of being secured in position with the hatch open or shut and shall be secured to the yacht by lanyard or other mechanical

6.52 Soft wood plugs, tapered and of various sizes.

6.53 *Ballast and Heavy Equipment.* Inside ballast in a yacht shall be securely fastened in position. All other heavy internal fittings (such as batteries, stoves, gas bottles, tanks, engines, out-board motors, etc.) and anchors and chains (see 8.31 and 8.32) shall be securely fastened against a capsize.

6.54 *Sheet winches* shall be mounted in such a way that no operator is required to be substantially below deck.

6.6 Lifelines, stanchions and pulpits

6.61 *For all yachts*

6.61.1 *Life-line terminals.* A taut lanyard of synthetic rope may be used to secure life-lines, provided that when in position its length does not exceed 4 ins. (10 cm).

6.61.2 *Stanchions shall* not be angled from the point of their attachment to the hull at more than ten degrees from vertical throughout their length.

6.62.3 *Overlapping pulpits.* Life-lines need not be affixed to the bow pulpit if they terminate at, or pass through, adequately braced stanchions 2 ft. (60 cm) (18 ins. (45 cm) for yachts under 21 feet R (28 feet/8.53m lenght overall) above the working deck, set inside and overlapping the bow pulpit, provided that the gap between the upper life-line and the bow pulpit does not exceed 6 ins. (15 cm).

6.61.4 *Pulpit and stanchion fixing.* Pulpits and stanchions shall be through-bolted or welded, and the bases thereof shall not be further inboard from the edge of the working deck than 5% of B max. (maximum beam) or 6 ins. (15 cm), whichever is greater. Stanchion bases shall not be situated outboard of the working deck.

6.62 *For yachts of 21 feet R (28 feet/8.53m length overall) and over.*

6.62.1 *Taut double life-lines,* with upper life-line of wire at a height of not less than 2 ft. (60 cm) above the working deck, to be permanently supported at intervals of not more than 7 ft. (2.15m). When the cockpit opens aft to the sea, additional life-lines must be fitted so that no opening is greater in height than 22 ins. (56 cm).

6.62.2 *Pulpits.* Fixed bow pulpit (forward of headstay) and stern pulpit (unless life-lines need not extend through the bow pulpit. Upper rails of pulpits shall be at not less height above the working deck than upper life-lines. Upper rails in bow pulpits shall be securely closed while racing.

Any lifeline attachment point will be considered as a stanchion in so far as its base shall not be situated outboard of the working deck.

6.63 *For yachts under 21 feet R (28 feet/8.53m length overall).*

6.63.1 *Taut single wire life-line,* at a height of not less than 18 ins. (45 cm) above the working deck, to be permanently supported at intervals of not more than 7 ft. (2.15m). If the life-line is at any point more than 22 ins. (56 cm) above the rail cap, a second intermediate life-line must be fitted. If the cockpit opens aft to the sea additional life-lines must be fitted so that no opening is greater in height than 22 ins. (56 cm).

6.63.2 *Pulpits.* Fixed bow pulpits and stern pulpit (unless life-lines are arranged as to adequately substitute for a stern pulpit). Lower life-lines need not extend through the bow pulpit. Upper rails of pulpits must be at no less height above the working deck than upper life-lines. Upper rails in bow pulpits shall be securely closed while racing. The bow pulpit may be fitted abaft the forestay with its bases secured at any points on deck, but a point on its upper rail must be within 16 ins. (40 cm) of the forestay on which the foremost headsail is hanked. Any life-line attachment point will be considered as a stanchion so far as its base shall not be situated outboard of the working deck.

6.64 *Toe Rails.* A toe-rail of not less than 1 in. (2.5 cm) shall be permanently fitted around the deck forward of the mast, except in way of fittings. Location to be not further inboard from the edge of the working deck than one third of the local beam.

A third life-line (or second for yachts under 21 ft. R (28 feet/8.53m length overall) at a height of not less than 1 in. (2.5 cm) or more than 2 ins. (5 cm) above the working deck will be accepted in place of a toe-rail.

7.0 Accommodations

7.11 *Toilet,* securely installed.

7.2 *Bunks, securely installed.*

7.31 *Cooking stove,* securely installed against a capsize with safe accessible fuel shutoff control capable of being safely operated in a seaway.

7.41 *Galley facilities,* including sink.

7.52 At least one securely installed water tank.

7.53 At least 2 gallons (9 litres) of water for emergency use carried in one or more separate containers.

8.0 General equipment

8.1 *Fire extinguishers,* at least two, readily accessible in suitable and different parts of the boat.

8.21.1 *Bilge Pumps,* at least two manually operated, securely fitted to the yacht's structure, one operable above, the other below deck. Each pump shall be operable with all cockpit seats, hatches and companionways shut.

8.21.2 *Each bilge pump shall be provided with permanently fitted discharge pipe(s) of sufficient capacity to accommodate simultaneously both pumps.*

8.21.3 *No bilge pumps may discharge into a cockpit unless that cockpit opens aft to the sea. Bilge pumps shall not be connected to cockpit drains.*

8.21.4 *Unless permanently fitted, each bilge pump handle shall be provided with a lanyard or catch or similar device to prevent accidental loss.*

8.24 *Two buckets of stout construction each with at least 2 galls. (9 litres) capacity. Each bucket to have a lanyard.*

8.31 *Anchors.* Two with cables except yachts rating under 21 feet R (28 feet/8.53m length overall) which shall carry at least one anchor and cable.

Anchors and any chain shall be securely fastened.

8.41 *Flashlights,* one of which is suitable for signalling, water resistant, with spare batteries and bulbs.

8.5 *First aid kit* and manual.

8.6 *Foghorn.*

8.7 *Radar reflector.* If a radar reflector is octahedral it must have a minimum diagonal measurement of 18 ins. (46 cm), or if not octahedral must have a documented 'equivalent echoing area' of not less than 10m^2.

8.9 *Shutoff valves* on all fuel tanks.

9.0 Navigation equipment

9.1 *Compass,* marine type, properly installed and adjusted.

9.1 *Spare compass.*

9.3 *Charts, light list and piloting equipment.*

9.5 *Radio direction finder.*

9.6 *Lead line or echo sounder.*

9.7 *Speedometer or distance measuring instrument.*

9.8 *Navigation lights,* to be shown as required by the International Regulations for Preventing Collision at Sea, mounted so that they will not be masked by sails or the heeling of the yacht.

Yachts under 7m LOA shall comply with the regulations for those between 12m and 7m LOA (i.e. they shall exhibit sidelights and a sternlight).

Navigation lights shall not be mounted below deck level. Spare bulbs for navigation lights shall be carried.

10.0 Emergency equipment

10.1 *Emergency navigation lights* and power source. Emergency navigation lights shall not be used if the normal navigation lights (under Rule 9.8) are operable.

10.21 *The following specifications for mandatory sails give maximum areas; smaller areas may well suit some yachts.*

10.21.1 *One storm trysail* not larger than 0.175 P × E in area. It shall be sheeted independently of the boom and shall have neither a headboard nor battens and be of suitable strength for the purpose. The yacht's sail number and letter(s) shall be placed on both sides of the trysail in as large a size as is practicable.

10.21.2 *One storm jib* of not more than 0.05 IG^2 (5% height of the foretriangle squared) in area, the luff of which does not exceed 0.65 IG (65% height of the foretriangle), and of suitable strength for the purpose.

10.21.3 *One heavy-weather jib* of suitable strength for the purpose with area not greater than 0.135 IG^2 (13.5% height of the foretriangle squared) and which does not contain reef points.

10.23 Any storm or heavy-weather jib if designed for a seastay or luff-groove device shall have an alternative method of attachment to the stay or a wire luff.

10.24 No mast shall have less than two halyards each capable of hoisting a sail.

10.3 *Emergency steering equipment*

10.31 An emergency tiller capable of being fitted to the rudder stock.

10.32 Crews must be aware of alternative methods of steering the yacht in any sea condition in the event of rudder failure. An inspector may require that this method be demonstrated.

10.4 *Tools and spare parts,* including adequate means to disconnect or sever the standing rigging from the hull in the case of need.

10.5 *Yacht's name* on miscellaneous buyoyant equipment, such as life jackets, oars, cushions, et. Portable sail number.

10.61 *Marine radio transitter and receiver.* If the regular antenna depends upon the mast, an emergency antenna must be provided.

Yachts fitted with VHF transceivers are recommended to instal VHF Channel 72 (156.625 MHz Simplex). This is an international ship-ship channel which, by "common use", could become an accepted yacht-yacht channel for all ocean racing yachts anywhere in the world.

10.62 *Radio receiver* capable of receiving weather bulletins.

11.0 Safety equipment

11.1 *Life jackets,* one for each crew member.

11.2 *Whistles* attached to life jackets.

11.3 *Safety belt* (harness type) one for each crew member.

Each yacht may be required to demonstrate that two thirds of the crew can be adequately attached to strong points on the yacht.

11.41 *Life rafts(s)*** capable of carrying the entire crew and meeting the following requirements:

A Must be carried on the working deck or in a special stowage opening immediately to the working deck containing the life-raft(s) conly.

B For yachts built after 1.7.83

Life-raft(s) may only be stowed under the working deck provided:
a the stowage compartment is watertight or self draining.
b if the stowage compartment is not watertight, then the floor of the special stowage is defined as the cockpit sole for the purposes of rule 6.23.2
c the cover of this compartment shall be capable of being opened under water pressure.

C Life-raft(s) packed in a valise and not exceeding 40kg may be securely stowed below deck adjacent to the companionway.

D Each raft shall be capable of being got to the lifelines within 15 seconds.

E Must be designed and used solely for saving life at sea.

F Must have at least two separate buoyancy compartments, each of which must be automatically inflatable; each raft must be capable of carrying its rated capacity with one compartment deflated.

G Must have a canopy to cover the occupants.

H Must have a valid annual certificate from the manufacturer or an approved servicing agent certifying that is has been inspected, that it complies with the above requirements and stating the official capacity of the raft which shall not be exceeded. The certificate, or a copy thereof, to be carried on board the yacht.

I Must have the following equipment appropriately secured to each raft:
   Sea anchor or drogue
1 Bellows, pump or other means for maintaining inflation of air chambers
1 Signalling light
3 Hand flares
1 Baler
1 Repair Kit
2 Paddles
1 Knife

J Provision for emergency water and rations to accompany rafts in waterproof, buoyant grab bags. (See ORC Recommended Standard Specifications for list of recommended minimum contents.)

11.52 At least one horseshoe-type life-ring equipped with a drogue and a self-igniting light having a duration of at least 45 minutes within reach of the helsman and ready for instant use.

11.53 At least one more horseshoe-type life-ring equipped with a whistle, dye marker, drogue, a self-igniting high-intensity water light, and a pole and flag. The pole shall be permanently extended and attached to the ring with 25 ft. (8m) of floating line and is to be of a length and so ballasted that the flag will fly at least 6ft. (1.8m) off the water.

11.61 *Distress signals* to be stowed in waterproof container(s), and meeting the following requirements for each category, as indicated:

11.63 Four red parachute flares.

11.64 Four red hand flares.

11.65 Four white hand flares.

11.66 Two orange smoke day signals.

11.7 *Heaving line* (50 ft. (16m) minimum length) readily accessible to cockpit.

Index

The unique international "This is . . ." series in
full colour throughout

This is Sailing
Richard Creagh-Osborne
New edition revised by Steve Sleight
The world's established primer of basic sailing with more than a quarter
of a million copies sold.

This is Racing
Richard Creagh-Osborne
What to do on the race course: how to enjoy the race and how to win it.

This is Down Wind Sailing
John Oakeley
How to cope with modern down wind sails: spinnakers, their gear
and handling.

The Colour Book of Knots
Floris Hin
The knot book with a difference. Bends, hitches, splices and whippings:
every strand shown in a different colour.

This is Sailboat Cruising
J.D. Sleightholme
How to handle and make passages in a small yacht: almost a practical
voyage with its full colour realism.

This is Rough Weather Cruising
Erroll Bruce
Exactly what to do and what to expect when the wind rises to 25 knots
or even higher.

This is Board Sailing
Uwe Farke, Volker Mohle, Detlef Schroder
Board sailing for beginners showing the new generation techniques in
colour pictures.

This is Boat Handling at Close Quarters
Dick Everitt and Rodger Witt
Coping with all conditions in different kinds of craft, in harbours,
anchorages and marinas.